DECODING THE LOST WORLD OF THE MAYA

A Personal Odyssey

Lindsay McAuley

Published in Australia in 2020 by Lindsay McAuley

Email: Lfaraway@bigpond.com
Website: www.lindsaymcauley.com

© Lindsay McAuley 2020

The moral right of the author has been asserted.

All rights reserved.

No part of this publication may be reproduced, stored in a retrieval system, or transmitted in any form or by any means, electronic, mechanical, photocopying, recording, or otherwise, without prior written permission from the author.

ISBN 9780980697551 (paperback)
       9780980697568 (hardback)

A catalogue record for this book is available from the National Library of Australia

Disclaimer

The author has made every effort to ensure the accuracy of the information within this book was correct at the time of publication. The author does not assume and hereby disclaims any liability to any party for any loss, damage or disruption caused by errors or omissions, whether such errors or omissions result from accident, negligence, or any other cause.

Contents

List of Illustrations and Tables v
    Images   v
    Maps   vii
    Diagrams   vii
    Tables   x

Preface xiii

Introduction 1
    Measuring the Vibe   1
    Digital Measurement   4

Chapter 1: Becoming Them 9
    The Temple Landscape   10
    A Historical Perspective   13
    The Maya Landscape of Time   18
    Parallels Within Cycles   21
    The Days of the Calendar   23

Chapter 2: The Defining Measurement 28
    Measuring the World   29
    One Step at a Time   31
    The Lost Tribe Pathway   40

Chapter 3: Measuring the Invisible 43
    The Number System   44
    The Golden Ratio   46
    Making the Invisible, Visible   48

Chapter 4: I Was Here 71
    The Hypothetical of the Ark, the Rod and the Boat 73
    The Historical Value of Measurement 83
    The Star of David and the Seal of Solomon 86
    Who Was Here? 98
    The Temple of Solomon 99

Chapter 5: The Neurotransmitter Fix 102
    Regional Guatemala 108
    The Steel Is Tempered in the Mud 111
    Serotonin 123
    Why Maria? 126
    Last Chance 128

Chapter 6: Temporary Residence 132
    Inflicted Conflict 135

Chapter 7: Under a Starless Sky 140
    The Unexpected Zodiac 142
    Dementia on the Caribbean 148

Chapter 8: Remembering, Not Analysing 161
    Time Travelling or Remembering? 162
    Science, Metaphysics or Philosophy: Which Way? 168
    Skyharp 172

Chapter 9: Is this the Warning of the Art of Aquarius? 175
    A Collaboration Between Civilisations 175
    What Was Once Concealed Will Be Revealed 179

Epilogue: Now 190

Glossary of Terms 192

References 195

Appendix 201

Acknowledgements and Image Credits 205

About the Author 207

List of Illustrations and Tables

Images

Image 1: CyArk 3-dimensional lidar image of the Temple of Kukulkan

Image 2: The Temple of Kukulkan, Yucatán Peninsula, Mexico

Image 3: El Caracol, an astronomy observatory at Chichen Itza, Mexico

Image 4: Sculptured heads, possibly representing the deity Kukulkan

Image 5: A crowd waits for the appearance of the shadow during the equinox

Image 6: Early photograph of the Temple of Kukulkan (taken by Teobert Maler, 1892)

Image 7: Olmec colossal head sculpture

Image 8: The Dresden Codex, also known as the *Codex Dresdensis* (replica housed in Museo Regional de Antropología, Villahermosa, Mexico)

Image 9: Egyptian cubit rod in the Liverpool World Museum (photograph by Dave Lightbody)

Image 10: The base of the west-facing stairway

Image 11: The height of each step at Kukulkan

Image 12: Encoded within the architecture of the Temple of Kukulkan are the fluid cycles of time5

Image 13: The stone border around the perimeter of the pyramid

Image 14: The temple on the elevated platform

Image 15: Artistic representation of Solomon's Temple, 10th century BCE (illumination by Jean Fouquet from a 15th century French edition of Flavius Josephus's *Antiquities of the Jews*)

Image 16: Ancient ruins with the city of Tunis in the background, Tunisia, North Africa

Image 17: The *Phoenicia* off the Mediterranean coast of Tunisia

Image 18: The *Phoenicia* moored in Tunisia

Image 19: The height of the steps on the Temple of Kukulkan in spans and cubits

Image 20: Egyptian royal cubit, Department of Egyptian Antiquities, Louvre Museum

Image 21: The riser and tread combined measure as one cubit

Image 22: The stele of the Code of Hammurabi (Babylon) depicts the king holding what may be interpreted as a measurement rod

Image 23: The Star of David and the Seal of Solomon

Image 24: The stone border around the perimeter of the temple

Image 25: The main temple on the elevated platform

Image 26: Late afternoon, Tikal, Guatemala

Image 27: Yaxhá Lake is situated in northern Petén, Guatemala

Image 28: Classic Maya pyramid, Yaxhá

Image 29: The author measuring steps in the ruins of Guatemala

Image 30: Flores is a town situated on an island in Guatemala's northern Petén region

Image 31: The Guatemalan public transport known locally as a chicken bus

Image 32: A typical house with thatched roof in regional Guatemala

Image 33: Laundry day at a nearby creek

Image 34: The mule and guide walking through the mud and slush

Image 35: One of the largest pyramids in the world, La Danta pyramid in northern Guatemala

Image 36: The thick rainforest where an ancient civilisation once thrived at El Mirador, abandoned almost 2000 years ago

Image 37: Detailed artwork from a lost civilisation

Image 38: A howler monkey rests in the forest canopy

Image 39: My travelling companions

Image 40: A photograph of an orb, with enlargement

Image 41: Fresh jaguar footprint in the mud

Image 42: Temple 1 in Tikal is approximately 47 metres high

Image 43: Sacred ceiba tree

Image 44: An ocellated turkey

Image 45: Fuego Volcano activity, south-western Guatemala

Image 46: Indigenous Maya girl, Maria Ac Pop

Image 47: Three little pigs

Image 48: A green-billed toucan reaches for a berry

Image 49: Palenque ruins, Mexico

Image 50: A design feature in the architecture at Palenque known as a tau cross

Image 51: Measuring the tau cross, which equals approximately one cubit

Image 52: A Chac Mool statue, photographed at Chichen Itza, Mexico

Image 53: Maya ceremony at Tikal, Guatemala (photograph by Jerson Gonzalez)

Image 54: The arrival of the *Phoenicia* in the Dominican Republic after crossing the Atlantic Ocean

Image 55: Columbus may have had an affection for pigeons, yet he developed a strong dislike for the local Taíno population

Image 56: Domed ceiling in the Dominican Convent with 32 rays emanating from the centre, most likely representing the 32nd degree of the Masonic order

Image 57: Sunset over the Caribbean

Image 58: The sails of the *Phoenicia*

Image 59: The toilet

Image 60: Captain Philip Beale at the helm on board the Phoenicia

Image 61: Below deck in the sleeping quarters

Image 62: Chart showing the way through the Windward Passage

Image 63: A storm gathers

Image 64: *Skyharp* art sculpture showing irregular shadow patterns on the background

Image 65: *Skyharp* art sculpture showing aligned circles during equinox

Image 66: Tourists viewing the Temple of Kukulkan

Maps

Map 1: Map of Mexico showing the location of Chichen Itza and the Temple of Kukulkan

Map 2: Guatemala and surrounding countries

Map 3: Tunis, Tunisia

Map 4: Map of Guatemala showing location of Flores and El Mirador

Map 5: The journey of the *Phoenicia* from Tunisia to the Dominican Republic and on to Miami, Florida, USA

Diagrams

Diagram 1: Shadow on descending stairway (artistic impression)

Diagram 2: The Temple of Kukulkan showing relative day-length dimensions

Diagram 3: Temple of Kukulkan site reference map

Diagram 4: The numerical Maya counting system

Diagram 5: The golden ratio 1.618

Diagram 6: The comparative relationship between a circle and the plan of the Temple of Kukulkan

Diagram 7: The distance between the east and west stair stringers

Diagram 8: Plan view of temple showing 262 mm or one day either side

Diagram 9: The comparative length of a chord determining the width of the steps

Diagram 10: Using the Pythagorean theorem, the hypotenuse equals 260 days

Diagram 11: One of the four stairways on the Temple of Kukulkan, each with 91 steps

List of Illustrations and Tables

Diagram 12: Hypothetical diagonal length equal to the 365-day Haab

Diagram 13: The height to the top of the temple measured in days

Diagram 14: The dimensions of the Temple of Kukulkan and its relationship to the golden ratio (1.618) and the $\sqrt{5}$ (2.236)

Diagram 15: The dimensions of the Temple of Kukulkan and its relationship to Venus and Mercury

Diagram 16: The circumference is equal to the 365-day Haab

Diagram 17: The mean length of the base of the temple corresponds to the 210-day cycle

Diagram 18: The dimensions of the stone border

Diagram 19: The plan view relative to the elevation showing the golden ratio

Diagram 20: Detail of proposed intended dimensions of the stairway area

Diagram 21: Various day-length dimensions represented in the Temple of Kukulkan in plan and elevation views

Diagram 22: The Temple of Kukulkan showing the relative day-lengths

Diagram 23: Elevation and plan views showing dimensions in spans and cubits

Diagram 24: Calculations derived from an inscribed six-pointed star enclosed within a circle with a circumference of 819 days

Diagram 25: The length of the side of each triangle corresponds to the length of the stone border surrounding the temple

Diagram 26: The side lengths of the temple base correspond with the length of a line where it intersects with the circle

Diagram 27: The width of the elevated platform is almost the same as the intersecting points within a six-pointed star

Diagram 28: The width of the steps is exactly half the height of the small triangles

Diagram 29: The overall height and the height to the elevated platform correspond to measurements within a six-pointed star

Diagram 30: This composite diagram shows how the six-pointed star relates to the dimensions of the Temple of Kukulkan

Diagram 31: Solomon's Temple possible internal length as compared to the height of the Temple of Kukulkan

Diagram 32: Detail of stairway showing relationship of smaller measurements to the whole

Diagram 33: The Temple of Kukulkan's design accurately reflects the proportional size ratio of the earth to the moon

Diagram 34: *Skyharp* sculpture showing earth-to-moon size ratio

Diagram 35: Cover design showing earth-to-moon ratio

Diagram 36: A 3-dimensional tetrahedron

Diagram 37: Two tetrahedrons combined comprise what is known as a Merkabah

Diagram 38: A 3-dimensional tetrahedron showing four corners and four sides

Diagram 39: Proposed 3-dimensional tetrahedron superimposed on the Temple of Kukulkan

Tables

Table 1: Temple of Kukulkan dimensions converted from metres to days

Table 2: Temple of Kukulkan pyramid base side lengths converted from metres to days

Table 3: Temple of Kukulkan pyramid base side lengths converted from metres to days

Table 4: Comparison of Temple of Kukulkan measurements with six-pointed star measurements

Table A1: 819-day Maya calendar temple reference and comparative values

Table A2: 365-day Maya calendar temple reference and comparative values

Table A3: 260-day Maya calendar temple reference and comparative values

Table A4: 210-day Maya calendar temple reference and comparative values

List of Illustrations and Tables

Table A5: 117-day Maya calendar temple reference and comparative values

Table A6: Summary of Maya calendar comparative values and error margins

Preface

Standing at the base of one of the New Seven Wonders of the World, I experienced a strange feeling. Somehow, I had a sense I knew what had happened there thousands of years earlier. I had a perception, although somewhat vague, about the foundation behind the design. I knew what lay mathematically underneath the facade of stone. Mysteriously, I felt I had either lived there at some point in the distant past or been transported back through time unconsciously.

To this day I cannot explain how all this came about. I am still without the full complement of words to describe the sensation. What started out as a routine holiday to Mexico for my wife and me rapidly turned into a life-changing journey of altered consciousness for myself. Since then, I have been remembering my way back little by little. Without a doubt, I know I have been part of a miraculous process.

I soon found myself on the pathway of documenting my experience. I never dreamed, even as recently as two years before this book was published, that I would be writing about Mesoamerican history or exploring ancient biblical events. My predominant interests are art and astronomy, and yet, from somewhere out of the blue, this book has arrived. It certainly has taken me on a journey, mentally, physically and spiritually.

You are invited to come with me through several countries and two continents as I travel into the distant past. I search for a lost tribe that I never knew I was looking for until information came to me of their possible existence. This involved a 91-kilometre trek through the jungles of Guatemala, a trip to North Africa, and then a cruise across the Caribbean on a 2600-year-old Phoenician replica sailing ship. Still further, I travel deep within the recesses of memory. All this, then to be handed a message by an unexpected chance encounter from someone who gave me a reminder of how life should be lived. This is one of life's greatest lessons, medically proven, scientifically sound, and which I have as a gift to share with you.

To some extent, I believe much of this work is born of some kind of psychic phenomena. Should I say divine intervention? Perhaps not. I will leave you to be the judge of that. Definitely, providence was at work behind the scenes.

After about a year of intense mathematical analysis and geometric interpretation, my initial intuitive hunch is confirmed. With 99.5% accuracy, I am now able to calculate various time periods from the Maya calendar that are concealed in the ratios and proportions of the Temple of Kukulkan at Chichen Itza, Mexico. This proves there was a complex intelligence at work with a clear intent behind the design. It is already understood the ancient Maya were capable mathematicians and astronomers.

Equally significant, and controversial to say the least, is what lies at the heart of the design foundation of this ancient landmark. I have discovered a geometric symbol or, more accurately, I should say it has been revealed to me. This image seems so mysteriously out of place with the local culture, yet is mathematically aligned perfectly with the architecture. It almost defies logic. My research suggests there was a collaboration between two distinct ancient civilisations, one from across the Atlantic Ocean.

The means to explore connections between ancient Maya architecture and Mediterranean mysticism is mathematics. I have acquired a reasonable skill at this discipline via a sudden and steep learning curve over recent years. The mathematics of measurement is the anchor holding this story together. Attempts to prove archaeological evidence or theories are often vigorously contested as being subjective, speculative or anecdotal. However, it is difficult to argue with numbers that have their own built-in defence mechanism. If it adds up, then it adds up. End of argument.

In this book, you will discover the extreme lengths I went to and understand why I felt compelled to document this information. There were several challenges I had to overcome to bring this book into reality. Firstly, my family, who all thought I had gone a bit strange—they already know I am different. Next was the isolation of writing on this subject with nobody in my vicinity who had similar interests—several friends tested my resolve by questioning who would be interested in this content and why would I bother troubling myself. Finally, these hurdles were minor compared with my own struggle wondering if it were true. Had I really gone a bit strange? This is the reason I have "personal odyssey" in the book's title.

I believe without a doubt this research significantly enriches our current understanding of the intellectual capacity of the ancient Maya. As well, this book provides the strongest evidence to date of foreign influence in pre-Columbian Mesoamerican history.

Lindsay McAuley

Introduction

Measuring the Vibe

The UNESCO World Heritage–listed Temple of Kukulkan at Chichen Itza on the Yucatán Peninsula in Mexico was in front of me in all its geometric perfection. The heat was almost as oppressive as the security guard assigned to guide us as we lugged our camera equipment around the archaeological site. I had planned to get some archival footage while there. "No commentary" was the order of the day. *Sin commentaries.* Just general shots. I was not allowed to stand in front of the camera on a tripod and deliver any dialogue with Chichen Itza archaeology in the background. But I noticed an inconsistency with what was happening around me. Hundreds of people were walking around talking to their smartphones without interruption. Coming from a country like Australia where freedom of speech is a core attribute, I wondered about the reasoning behind the obsessive restrictions placed on me. This was even after paying over A$1000 to the relevant government historical authorities in order to film within the archaeological zone.

I wanted a little space to experience the place on my own. A plan was hatched to counter this limitation. If I kept up a steady, relentless pace, surely I could wear out our attached mentor and he would have to head back to the air-conditioned office for a siesta. I was 60 and he was about 25 years old. Quite rapidly that tactic failed miserably. He stuck to us like the heavy humid atmosphere. There was no escape from either.

Perhaps the only valid perspective that has credibility is from the university-educated archaeologists who have navigated Maya history. What I have to say as a visual artist really does not fit well with their selection criteria. I understand that. The correct information should be told to the public by those who have studied the subject. However, I believe there should be room for new information outside of this status quo. But time-travel experience does not go down well on the curriculum vitae. Someone who is a bit left-field, one of those artistic types, having only spent 10 days at Chichen Itza suddenly becomes an authority on Maya archaeology? Perhaps not. I resigned myself to the fact this was not my country and I should abide by its laws, even though I was not entirely pleased.

The Maya civilisation and their contribution to science, astronomy and art is of universal significance and should not be parochial or limited to one particular field of study. My opinion is that my opinion is equally as valid as someone else's.

The 21 December 2012 end-of-the-world prophecy related to the Maya calendar turned into a publicity event in the media. Cataclysm is a very marketable word as we enter this new millennium. Nothing significant happened on that day that we are aware of; however, it is arguable that the world is now on the verge of dramatic change, socially, politically and environmentally. The widespread media publicity of the Maya calendar outside academia suggests that non-academic theories do have some value.

I just wanted to measure the temple, but my tape remained in my luggage unused. So, I had another idea. I would become like water. If I met resistance anywhere during this process, I would just move around any obstacles in my way. Circumstances might slow me down, but this investigation would not be stopped. If I met an almost impenetrable wall, I would use the process of osmosis to get through. I would find a way to measure the temple one way or another. Tenacity is part of my make-up.

Upon my return to Australia, I was having second thoughts. I felt reluctant to go any further with this. However, it would not leave me alone. I paced the floor indecisively for about a week before fully embracing this project. I knew what hard work would be involved, what level of resources it would take to do this right. Will I sacrifice the next few years to this epic journey? Will I, or won't I?

The Temple of Kukulkan had already been measured, but not very well. Not comprehensively enough for what I needed to know and with a variety of different results. I didn't want to rely on the inaccuracy of internet sites using words like "about" 30 metres high, "almost" 53 metres wide. I wanted perfection. Providence became my friend.

The Temple of Kukulkan had been scanned using lidar (light detection and ranging) laser equipment by an organisation called CyArk. This non-profit organisation, founded in 2003, records archaeological sites for posterity, storing the information digitally. That up-to-date lidar data was accessible to the public online. Just down the road from where I lived in Australia, I found the solution. Less than 5 kilometres away, a manager of a land survey company was kind enough to allow me the use of their technician, who was skilled at analysis of 3-dimensional scans. I could now measure the temple to within an error of 10–20 millimetres (mm) while sitting in an air-conditioned studio. This was operating in an alternative reality, similar to my experience in time travel on my recent trip to Mexico, a digital environment that was real and yet not really real. An error margin of 10–20 mm over 68.1 m; that type of accuracy I can accept.

By remote control from halfway around the world, I had stumbled across a measurement system used by the Maya builders over a thousand years earlier, something a university professor of archaeology would hope and pray for after traipsing through the jungle for 40 years. Using lidar technology, the Temple of Kukulkan can now be measured properly by anyone, probably for the first time since it was built between the 4th and 8th centuries CE.

Had I been allowed to measure the Temple of Kukulkan using my relative inexperience as a surveyor, I could never have achieved the accuracy that was possible using the 3-dimensional lidar scans produced by CyArk (Image 1). Lidar scans use a pulse from a laser to collect measurements. This system is a sophisticated remote-sensing technology that uses laser light to sample data. Millions of laser pulses are beamed at an object from the ground or by aerial photography. The highly accurate measurements are then used to produce a detailed 3-dimensional image of the ground surface topography; 3-dimensional models and maps of the environment can be created from this digital information. It was this technology that uncovered hundreds, perhaps thousands, of hidden temples in Guatemala previously thought to be just hills and vegetation. Used by surveyors, it is probably the most advanced and accurate up-to-date technology available, which allowed me to investigate the dimensions of the temple. This was without the complexity and inefficiency of running around the site with a measuring tape.

Image 1: CyArk 3-dimensional lidar image of the Temple of Kukulkan

Digital Measurement

As part of my determination to maintain accuracy, all measurements referred to in this book are based on analysis of the CyArk lidar ground survey data.

Historically, all measurements on the temple were done through conventional architectural surveying techniques using either metric or imperial measures. This historical data is a valuable resource from which to do the conversion. However, there are limitations in accuracy when using traditional surveying techniques. The internet is an unreliable source of information because of the variations in the recording of mathematical data. As a result of these and other circumstances mentioned previously, I have searched for and found this more accurate, up-to-date method, which I believe provides the capability for anyone to independently obtain comprehensive measurements of the temple.

There is a reason I wanted to know the exact measurements. For one, I am a bit of a perfectionist. I do not like settling for inaccuracy. It annoys me when something is not done right. The other thing is the Maya builders were not rough and ready. I intuitively knew that before I measured the temple. Now, I know for certain. Accurate measurements were critical to helping me develop my understanding of the philosophy behind the design. This obsession was essential to support two of my proposed evidence-based theories:

- First, several time durations from the Maya calendar are encoded in the Temple of Kukulkan using ratio and proportion.
- Second, a six-pointed star was the basis of its design using an ancient measurement identical to that used in the Mediterranean region.

I believe I have proven these observations mathematically.

The following will help explain a relatively abstract, esoteric concept. It is concerned with the application of measurement using time as a reference.

Imagine you find yourself exploring the recesses of an ancient crypt, dark and mysterious, among the archaeology of an ancient civilisation. There you discover, concealed inside a sarcophagus, a measuring rod with numbers written in an unknown text. However, these numbers, marked sequentially, do not represent inches or a metric measurement. Nor do they appear to represent any other form of easily recognisable ancient measure. From your perspicacity in examining cryptology, you decipher that each demarcation represents a moment in time: the length of a day. You might wonder where on earth someone could use this strange kind of measuring system. Using the principles of time defined as a physical measurement must be an alien concept. It is totally abstract and virtually impossible to comprehend in its application. Time as a physical length, marked by the movement of the earth around the sun. Not inches. Not metres. Time. It may seem impossible to define a practical use for a physical measurement system such as this, the progression of planet earth around the sun counted in days as a measurement system.

How could this already abstract notion, time, be defined as a physical measurement? It can, and it is far less alien to the average person's understanding than first appears. I present the following as an example of how the concept is already deep within our conversational interaction.

In order to gauge distance, you might ask someone, "How far is it to Sydney from here?" An answer may come, depending on where the question is posed, "It's about a 2-day drive." You do a quick mental calculation, redefining the terminology. A 2-day drive must be recalculated into a sense of physical distance, thereby estimating a measurement in kilometres or miles. In effect, you have been given a time reference. They have given you the axis rotation of the earth from which to recalculate a physical measurement, the length in kilometres or miles from where you are in order to travel to Sydney. This communication style is similar to how that strange measurement rod found in the ancient crypt might be used.

It may come as a surprise that, unconsciously, we often employ a 2000-year-old technique of using time as a physical measurement to gauge distance. This is exactly the same method I believe the Maya from Central America used in the construction of one of their most enduring monuments at Chichen Itza: a measurement of time, interpreted as a physical distance. Inversely, a physical measure interpreted as time. This seemingly abstract concept is not unfamiliar to our current civilisation. How far is it to the bus station? It's about a 5-minute walk from here. To the local pub? About a 10-minute stroll depending on your level of thirst. These are all examples of a length of distance measured using a unit of time.

The Maya used this concept in a very special way. They harnessed the cycles of nature, using their calendar's qualities within architectural design. This was a way of maintaining a connection with their philosophy and way of life. Their built environment was a reflection of their calendar, the hallmark of their civilisation. In doing so, the surroundings communicated back to them in a way that was congruent with their worldview. They were as connected physically to their architecture in terms of ratio and proportion as they were intellectually to their cultural belief systems. Their calendar was conceived out of an observation of the qualities of time; translated as geometry and using mathematics, their architectural design was born of these same principles. Time is frozen in stone.

Time as a measurement system is already integrated in our dialogue. It is already part of our modern standard units of measure. Unconsciously, we have something in common with one of the most enigmatic, scientifically advanced civilisations to have ever walked the earth, the Maya.

Introduction

Image 2: The Temple of Kukulkan, Yucatán Peninsula, Mexico

Image 3: El Caracol, an astronomy observatory at Chichen Itza, Mexico

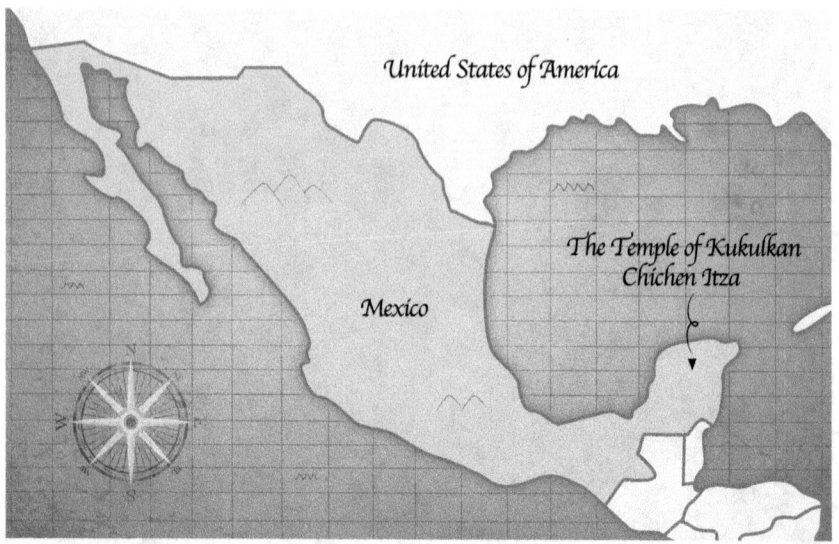

Map 1: Map of Mexico showing the location of Chichen Itza and the Temple of Kukulkan

Chapter 1

Becoming Them

What is the value of knowledge, without understanding?
—unknown

The Temple of Kukulkan in Mexico on the Yucatán Peninsula is an enigma. In fact, much of the Maya civilisation in general is difficult to comprehend from a modern point of view. Their lifestyle was bound by certain cultural priorities that seem alien to us. They lived by time. We do as well. However, we are forced to by the social conditioning and environment we live in. They perceived time from a religious, spiritual point of view. Each day was significant. Every day was numbered within a complex, intricate system of counting. This became known as the Maya calendar.

The Maya were meticulous in recording their scientific research concerning astronomy and mathematics. They had the future in mind. That's us. Now, we are the future looking back. From across the centuries, they are calling us so that we may remember what was forgotten. They are calling us at this pivotal time in history. Their voice can be heard if we listen carefully, if we tune our minds away from the iron grip the material world of fear has on all of us. We are called now to remember.

Investigating ancient Maya sites is usually the job of archaeologists and complementary professionals who have already deciphered their complex counting system and studied the Maya calendar. However, it takes more than objectivity to really understand them. We must think like them. We must become them, in a sense. Rather than a pick and a shovel, a sieve and a trowel, mathematics has been my archaeological tool. Mathematics was the perspective of the Maya's mystical worldview. That has been my challenge. That has been my preoccupation throughout writing this book: to walk in their shoes, to get inside their heads.

To get there, I have used a little bit of clairvoyance. I have raised my antenna and tuned in to another frequency, mostly unconsciously. Whoops, I said that word, "clairvoyance". Now I have lost 80 percent of my academic audience in one sentence. Well, that is okay with me. See you later. The Maya were a mystical people. They were of this world but not entirely in it. My view is if you are going to study the Maya, if you are inclined toward being a scholar in this particular field, you must become mystical like them. Otherwise, you run the risk of just being a satellite in orbit around the nucleus.

Easier said than done. Be careful. It is possible to lose yourself. Their worldview is profoundly different from ours. With the rewards also come the risks. Destabilising is one way of describing the feeling. Conflict is another characteristic of the adventure. You can be rocked totally off your axis. You must become two people, in a sense. You must learn to mow the lawn and study the universe at the same time if you are to survive.

To know them, you must become them. *They*—who are they? Are you sure you want to do this? Are you sure you want to enter the mind of the ancient Maya? Read on, brave soul.

The Temple Landscape

This book will make the temple even more of an enigma. My research concerns the methods by which the Maya incorporated time within architecture. They used a profound technique by integrating a physical linear measurement with their calendar.

The Temple of Kukulkan stands 30.4 m high. Not so huge when compared with other pyramids around the world. The Great Pyramid on the Giza Plateau in Egypt is almost five times its height. However, the temple's stature increases significantly when its mathematical properties become more apparent.

The temple is surrounded by various other architectural stone structures at Chichen Itza. Rather than a chaotic, random layout, the site suggests a well-planned design, with each building functioning separately yet holistically. We can only guess the connection each structure has with one another. It is conceivable they are bound within a complex dimensional relationship.

Perfectly symmetrical, Kukulkan is the largest temple at the site, where it is obvious there was an intent to make this building a showpiece of significance. A prominent Mesoamerican supernatural entity or deity, the feathered serpent Quetzalcoatl is featured as stone snake-head carvings, two of which are symmetrically placed at the bottom of the pyramid either side of the north-facing stairway (Image 4). These sculptures were widespread as far south as the Guatemalan Highlands, where they sometimes depicted human heads protruding from the mouth. Quetzalcoatl is known to the Maya as Kukulkan. Therefore, the temple is called Kukulkan by the Maya people. The pyramid is known to the Spanish as *El Castillo*, meaning "the castle".

Image 4: Sculptured heads, possibly representing the deity Kukulkan

This structure is a remarkable achievement on the part of the designers and builders. Its design is creative, intelligent and profound. It suggests a determination to communicate some deep connection with the movement of the heavens. One striking characteristic of the temple is its alignment with the sun. During the equinox, which occurs twice a year, the sun's rays cast triangular-shaped shadows along the side of a stairway. This creates the illusion of the body of a giant snake descending the elevated temple to connect with one of the snake heads at the base (Diagram 1).

Diagram 1: Shadow on descending stairway (artistic impression)

The Chichen Itza archaeological zone is a popular destination worldwide. According to figures from Statista (2019), over 2.7 million tourists visited the zone in 2018.

Walking around the site in the heat with hundreds of other people, one can only imagine the colour and pageantry that existed thousands of years ago (Image 5). For those visitors who have not travelled extensively, the Chichen Itza site may seem like an alien landscape. That's because it is an alien landscape mentally. The architecture of the temple is strikingly individualistic. To achieve this kind of symmetry in design, the architects of the day must have had an evolved understanding of mathematics and geometry.

Chapter 1 : Becoming Them

Image 5: A crowd waits for the appearance of the shadow during the equinox

The equinox feature alone would have taken considerable planning and artistic vision in orientation and design. The Maya's capacity to carry out this project successfully indicates a high degree of organisational capability. There is a definite sense of purpose behind the design and implementation. It is our obligation to discover the builders' original intent. Time has removed the people, yet the temple remains. We are left to decipher the ancient motivations behind those who built this remarkable work. I believe this can be achieved by studying the dimensions of this structure, one of the most amazing places of the ancient world still in existence. We need to remember our way back through the centuries.

But why bother? It is all in the past. All that happened a long time ago, and we now have more important things to think about, like money, for instance. Well, I believe the Maya have something important to say to us that we need to hear. But first, a little historical perspective.

A Historical Perspective

Chichen Itza was first visited by the Spanish conquistadors as early as the 15th century, soon after the arrival of the Italian navigator, Christopher Columbus. Several of its buildings were described in about 1566 by Diego de Landa, a bishop of the Roman Catholic Archdiocese of Yucatán. Its history, as far as detailed architectural description is concerned, begins properly with an American archaeologist, John Lloyd Stephens, and an Englishman, Frederick Catherwood. They visited the site in 1842. Stephens' book, entitled *Incidents of Travel in Central America, Chiapas and Yucatan*, which Catherwood illustrated, inspired considerable interest in Mesoamerican culture (Stephens, 1843).

Their work prompted further explorations of the Chichen Itza site by people such as Désiré Charnay, a surveyor, and Augustus Le Plongeon and his wife, Alice Dixon Le Plongeon. Another notable explorer was Alfred Maudslay, who, together with his wife Anne Maudslay, published a concise description and photographic record of the area in their book, *A glimpse at Guatemala, and Some Notes on the Ancient Monuments of Central America* (Maudslay & Maudslay, 1899/2011). In 1894, Edward Herbert Thompson purchased the ruins of Chichen Itza where, for over 30 years, he explored the ancient buildings. He shipped numerous artefacts to the Peabody Museum at Harvard University. In early 1925, the Carnegie Institution of Washington initiated a series of excavation and restoration projects at the site. Restoration projects carried out under the auspices of the Instituto Nacional de Antropología e Historia (2020), Mexico, continue to this day.

Image 6: Early photograph of the Temple of Kukulkan (taken by Teobert Maler, 1892)

Chapter 1 : Becoming Them

The true intent of the designers remains totally obscured without an understanding of the unit of measurement used at Chichen Itza. Without this intuitive insight, it may as well still be covered by foliage and undergrowth.

Of all the Mesoamerican civilisations, it is the Maya who have emerged from history with a reputation as the most skilled artists, advanced mathematicians and innovative engineers. Their culture was rich in the study of the cycles of the planets. They developed a method to predict astronomy cycles hundreds of years into the future. A refined and distinctive art form, including sculpture, was punctuated by their intricate sophisticated calendar. Thousands of years ago, their culture emerged in the regions we now call Mexico, Guatemala and Honduras. The Maya influence also extended to Belize in the west and as far south as El Salvador (Map 2).

Map 2: Guatemala and surrounding countries

At its peak, Central America was one of the most densely populated regions with the most culturally dynamic societies in the world. Besides the Maya, significant Mesoamerican civilisations included the Aztec, Itza, Toltec, Copán, Mintec and Olmec.

Although the Maya have received the credit for developing the calendar, its origin can be traced back much earlier to a different civilisation, the Olmec (Image 7). From as early as 1000 BCE to 400 BCE the Olmecs are considered to be the first Mesoamerican society to develop into a civilisation. Their presence influenced the Maya and the Aztecs as well as the Itza. It was the Maya who refined the calendar and applied their wisdom to mathematics, astronomy and architecture. Therefore, the Maya calendar is perhaps a work in progress. I suspect there are more things to discover about its mathematics, which is one of the reasons I decided to write this book.

Image 7: Olmec colossal head sculpture

Chichen Itza is considered by archaeologists to have been built as early as 400 CE, although there are conflicting accounts to say it was constructed much later, between 800 CE and 1200 CE. The UNESCO World Heritage List website states, "the dates for this settlement vary according to subsequent local accounts: one manuscript gives 415-35 A.D., while others mention 455 A.D." (UNESCO, n.d., para. 2). The name Chichen Itza is interpreted as meaning "water well of the witches or shaman". It is thought there were Toltec and Itza influences in the construction.

Regardless of what civilisation was involved in its design and construction, the Temple of Kukulkan stands today as a remarkable artistic and architectural achievement. It blends science and art using stone and rock … and time.

The use of geometry and mathematical ratios is not uncommon in the history of global architecture. It may be seen as a significant evolution from the construction of rudimentary dwellings that served primarily as protection from the elements. This development of human interaction with the built environment for reasons other than survival was a substantial leap forward in human history. The surroundings become much more than just a means of protecting community members. Ratio and proportion in design standards provide a basis to observe, interact and navigate a path among a human-made landscape. Architecture reflects values congruent with a localised spiritual philosophy. That becomes perceivable here in the Temple of Kukulkan, where I have found evidence of its designers encoding several calendar timeframes using mathematics.

Mathematics has had a definite link with architecture since antiquity. As a consequence, mathematics helps reflect the social values of a society. The pyramids in Egypt are an ideal example. Decorated with iconography, the pyramids were an unmistakable reminder for the population of the spiritual and religious belief systems prevalent at the time. In Greece, public buildings were an indicator of the social importance of mathematics and symmetry. The Roman architect Vitruvius stated in the 1st century BCE:

> Order gives due measure to the members of a work considered separately, and symmetrical agreement to the proportions of the whole. (Vitruvius, ca. 1st century BCE/1914, para. 2)

Architecture is influenced by and exists as an indicator of social values. Solomon's Temple in ancient Jerusalem is an example of how construction measurements perceived as having a divine origin should follow a certain design protocol. As people from different regions of the world move their way through the local design of temples and surroundings that reflect their culture, they also travel across a landscape of their own philosophy. At Chichen Itza, I believe this was established by way of physical ratio and proportion using the mathematics of a single scale measurement.

> The mother art is architecture. Without an architecture of our own we have no soul of our own civilization. (Frank Lloyd Wright, n.d.)

Still very much related to the environment, as it has been since antiquity, architecture also strives to address the societal climatic conditions wherever it is located. With buildings now reaching tremendous heights, architecture can be seen as an indicator of economic wealth, reflecting our present orientation toward materialism and competition. Where once a church stood in a dominant position, such as on a hilltop elevated above the rest of the town, now skyscrapers, icons of our civilisation, reach for the heavens.

For the people, a constructed environment can provoke thoughts either of transcendental concepts or of impersonal, transient impressions. Architecture can provide, for some individuals, a feeling of alienation within an economically diverse society such as ours, or alternatively, as in times past, it can stimulate a sense of belonging, of inclusion within the grand vision of the collective.

The Maya Landscape of Time

The grand vision of the collective was lost for the Maya people with the Spanish conquest of Mesoamerica. Intellectual and spiritual havoc was wrought upon the indigenous people by the forced imposition of an alternative belief system. In one night, a Catholic bishop, Diego de Landa, eradicated most of the Maya codices, which the Maya had maintained for centuries. According to de Landa:

> [The codices] ... contained "nothing in which there was not to be seen superstition and lies of the devil," [and] he ordered all of the books to be burned "... which [the Maya] regretted to an amazing degree and which caused them great affliction". (The Editors of Encyclopedia Britannica, 2020a, para. 4)

The Maya science and astronomy records documented meticulously for centuries were almost totally eradicated. With the annihilation of their comprehensive written record, it follows that the surviving population would become increasingly disconnected over time from the essential meaning of their architectural landscape.

What remains now is only the physical evidence of a few codices, sculptures and the existing temples reclaimed from the encroaching rainforest. Remarkably, from the small number of codices remaining, historians and archaeologists have been able to decipher the Maya counting system. From deciphering their architecture, we may also be able to rebuild an understanding of their philosophy. By studying the language of mathematics within temple design, I believe we can attempt to interpret the intention of the first designers.

Only four codices exist of which the authenticity is beyond doubt. They are named after the cities where they are now stored:

- the Dresden Codex (see Image 8), also known as the *Codex Dresdensis*
- the Madrid Codex, also known as the *Tro-Cortesianus*
- the Paris Codex, also known as the *Codex Peresianus*
- the Grolier Codex, also known as the *Sáenz Codex*, authenticated in 2015 and officially renamed in 2018 as the Maya Codex of Mexico or *Códice Maya de México*.

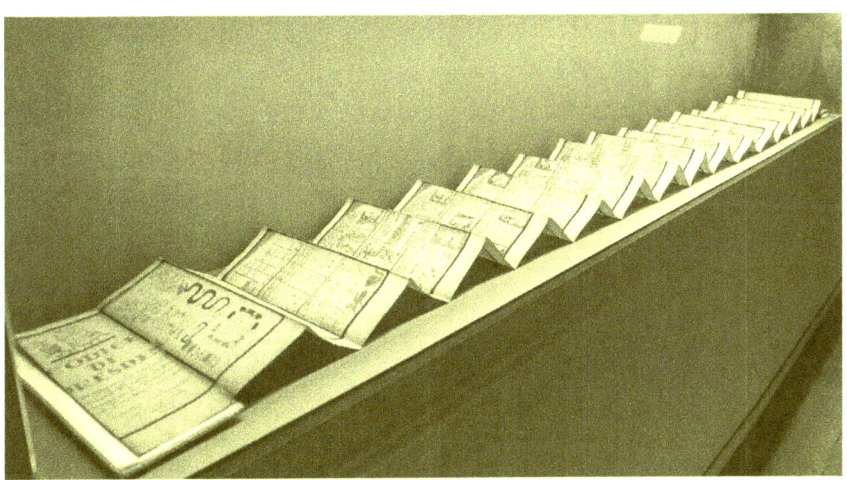

*Image 8: The Dresden Codex, also known as the **Codex Dresdensis** (replica housed in Museo Regional de Antropología, Villahermosa, Mexico)*

This background of loss and possible revival leads us to consider the Maya civilisation as one to which numerous accomplishments can be attributed. As well as being notable engineers and artists with an advanced numerical counting system, they were also skilled astronomers. We have learned through observation that the Maya created architecture oriented to view the sky based on celestial events. My research examines the possibility that their architecture stands as an intelligent confluence of geometry and their most salient belief system, their intricate and seemingly complex calendar. Their calendar was central to their worldview; therefore, it is perhaps logical to anticipate that the Maya designers would strive to imprint upon the architectural landscape an illustration of their time-keeping system. It is suggested here in this book that several calendrical numerical values were purposely encoded within ratio and proportion on this, one of their most important temples, the Temple of Kukulkan.

> A common assertion in traditional creation myths is that the Maker of the World first laid down a pattern of number from which all else proceeded. ... With this in mind, the ancient philosophers were concerned above all to seek out patterns in number which correspond to those in nature, and to set them up as models in the conduct of human affairs. (Michael, 1983, p. 121)

Because the Maya codices were destroyed by the Spanish, and consequently all possible evidence of the written use of geometry that they may have applied to architecture, attempts to revive the original intent of the designers remain largely anecdotal. However, I believe measurement is the means by which we can retrace the past. It allows us to follow an imaginary piece of string as if it had been attached to an anchor way back in ancient history.

By looking at the value systems still intact, as found in ritual ceremonies and creation narratives that have survived the destruction, it is possible to attempt to navigate our way back. For example, originally preserved through oral tradition, the *Popol Vuh* translates as the *Book of the People* and is a 2000-year-old creation narrative of the K'iche' people, who live predominantly in the Guatemalan Highlands. A cultural narrative that recounts mythology and history, it was first translated by an

18th-century Dominican friar, Francísco Ximénez, who made a copy of the original text in Spanish. It could be interpreted by examination of the following extract that Maya architectural dimension should follow a certain mathematical criterion:

> the fourfold siding, fourfold cornering,
> measuring, fourfold staking,
> halving the cord, stretching the cord
> in the sky, on the earth,
> the four sides, the four corners, as it is said,
> by the Maker, Modeler, …
> (D. Tedlock, 1996, pp. 63–64)

It is made relatively clear in ancient biblical text that construction should follow explicit design instructions such as for the building of Solomon's Temple in ancient Israel. I draw a comparison with these biblical protocols and the *Popol Vuh*. Similarly, the *Popol Vuh* may provide a record of ancient ancestral knowledge also suggesting design process should follow divine mystical instruction. In later chapters, I explore this text and its possible relationship to geometry and, therefore, to the design of the Temple of Kukulkan.

Parallels Within Cycles

In the lead up to 21 December 2012, a worldwide phenomenon was taking place. It was the calculated end-date of a 5126-year-long cycle in the Maya Long Count calendar equal to 13 cycles of b'ak'tun. The b'ak'tun is a time cycle in the Maya Long Count calendar consisting of 144,000 days, which is equal to 394.26 tropical years ("Baktun," 2020). The Maya believed the world began on 11 August 3114 BCE. The end of 13 of these b'ak'tun cycles coincided with the 2012 date, 5126 years later. A new cycle has now begun.

There were numerous interpretations of the ramifications of that date. Some believed 21 December 2012 would initiate the beginning of a new era, the start of a period during which the inhabitants of planet earth would undergo a spiritual transformation. Various astronomical alignments were proposed. Others suggested that the date marked the end of the world by a collision with a mythical planet, Nibiru. Academic Maya scholars, however, stated that there was no evidence to suggest impending doom or anything significant might occur.

The date came and went. The sun rose and set without interruption. The earth rotated on its axis as though oblivious to the concerns of some of its inhabitants. Because there were no obvious dramatic events to coincide with the end of the Maya cycle, subsequently it has become easy for people from various disciplines to reject the proposed doomsday scenarios as pseudoscience. The Maya cycle and its new-era connotations have lost some credibility. However, if we look at the world around us now, there may be some interesting parallels in science for us to consider.

A worldwide phenomenon was taking place within the scientific community concurrent with the end of the b'ak'tun cycle and still is. One major transitional event happened recently that has not happened before in the history of the earth as far as we know. It is the most significant event for the world to have occurred in the last 10,000 years geologically. There are implications for us and every other species on the planet.

In the year 2000, Nobel Laureate Paul J. Crutzen, vice-chair at the time of the International Geosphere Biosphere Program, and Eugene F. Stoermer, along with numerous other scientists, proposed that humanity had driven the world into a new geological epoch, "the Anthropocene". The Anthropocene epoch describes the relatively recent inability of the earth to regulate its natural functions as it did without interruption during the last epoch. This change has arisen from the direct impact of human activity. The expansion of humankind's population and exploitation of the earth's resources has been astounding in the last few decades. During the past three centuries, the human population has increased tenfold. In a few generations, humankind has almost exhausted the fossil fuels generated over several hundred million years. This rapid expansion of our presence has become a significant geological and morphological force affecting every aspect of the ecosystem, from biodiversity to the health of the atmosphere.

According to one of the 35 scientists who proposed the Anthropocene epoch, Alejandro Cearreta:

> Many of these changes have geological consequences, some of which are irreversible, says Cearreta. "It is a scientific fact that is being registered geologically," says Cearreta. "The Anthropocene evidence will be there forever." (Salas, 2016, para. 11)

Most scientists agree that the Anthropocene epoch is with us. However, assigning a specific date has raised varying viewpoints. Scientists are yet to place the metaphorical sword in the stone to designate a time reference for both the start of the new epoch and the end of the previous one. This comes about because there is no one identifiable cause that can be agreed upon unanimously; therefore, ratifying an exact date is difficult. The debate rages from atmospheric radioactivity caused by atomic bombs to the amount of microplastics in the environment. Should it start at the dawn of the industrial revolution? Is it this or is it that? Everybody is right, so everyone else is wrong. Most are in agreement that the topic has introduced some sense of urgency into addressing the world's environmental problems.

It might be true to say that some scientists have gone through a sort of spiritual transformation from the role of researcher to that of providing credible evidence of possible doomsday scenarios. There is just this issue of having a date that is the problem. If they could only agree and therefore give us a global geological birthday from which we could all recognise the beginning of the new epoch, would that give us reason to celebrate?

The coincidence of the beginning of a new geological epoch with the end of the Maya b'ak'tun cycle has been largely overlooked. The Maya mystics and shamans might be able to assist the scientists in identifying the date they are looking for from a holistic perspective rather than pinning it to one particular cause. If they were asked to contribute to the debate, I would say, as a pretty strong guess, the Maya would most likely identify the date for the beginning of the Anthropocene epoch as 21 December 2012.

The Days of the Calendar

The ancient Mesoamerican tribes' worldview was to venerate the movement of the sun, the moon and the planets. From this constant observation and a dedication to record-keeping, the Maya calendar, the hallmark of their civilisation, evolved. This system of recording the phenomena of astronomy time cycles is highly regarded for its remarkable accuracy and advanced complexity.

The Maya calendar operates in a cyclical manner with various shorter timeframes identified at certain points of reference within longer cycles. It is often depicted visually as a set of interlocking rotating cogs.

The most common description of the Maya calendar usually consists of a 260-day duration called the Tzolkin and a 365-day duration known as the Haab. Every 52 years, called the Calendar Round, the Tzolkin and the Haab are synchronised with each other. These two calendar durations are often called "sacred year" and "secular year" respectively. Other time durations specified include the following:

- k'in = 1 day
- uinal = 20 k'in = 20 days
- tun = 18 uinal = 360 days
- k'atun = 20 tun = 360 uinal = 7200 days
- b'ak'tun = 20 k'atun = 400 tun = 7200 uinal = 144,000 days.

In addition to the aforementioned calendrical timeframes, other time durations are also recognised as significant and are explained in more detail below. These day-length values serve as the primary reference in my research. It is these cycles that I believe underpin the entire design layout of the Temple of Kukulkan.

819-day cycle

This length seems ambiguous as it does not appear to coincide with any known planetary orbits. A reference to 819 days can be found in the Dresden Codex. It was significant to the Maya as it has shorter time periods of 7, 9 and 13 as factors:

819 days = 7 × 117 days, 9 × 91 days, or 13 × 63 days

Each consecutive group of 819 days was associated with one of four colours and the cardinal direction with which that colour was associated: black corresponded to west, red to east, white to north and yellow to south.

365-day cycle (Haab)

The 365-day cycle closely resembles the duration of our Gregorian calendar of 365.242 days. It is made up of 18 months of 20 days each, plus a period of 5 days ("nameless days") at the end of the year, known as Wayeb.

260-day cycle (Tzolkin)

By several accounts, the true origin of the Tzolkin 260-day cycle used by the Maya is largely unknown. The term Tzolkin, meaning "count of days", is considered to be a creation of modern researchers, sometimes referred to as Mayanists, those who study the Maya civilisation. The corresponding Postclassical Aztec calendar was called Tōnalpōhualli in the Nahuatl language. To save further confusion, I will use the term Tzolkin in reference to the 260-day calendar.

The Tzolkin or sacred calendar consists of a cycle of 20 named days combined with a cycle of 13 numbers (the trecena) to produce 260 unique days. The priests may have used the Tzolkin to determine specific days for harvest and religious ceremonies. In her 1983 book, *Time and the Highland Maya*, Barbara Tedlock says that, in the highlands of Guatemala, a 260-day period between planting and harvesting is still used.

In an online extract from his 1994 book, *Tzolkin: Visionary Perspectives and Calendar Studies*, John Major Jenkins writes:

> There are straightforward connections between the cycles of Venus, the moon and the tzolkin. For example, the 260-day cycle can be used to predict eclipses in the following way. Eclipses occur, on the average, every 173.33 days. This is known as the "eclipse half-year." Three of these equal 520 days, and this is exactly two tzolkins. ... Furthermore, Venus is visible as morning star for about 258 days. In general, the tzolkin is the key to a larger calendric system which can predict many astronomical cycles of the moon and planets. (Jenkins, 1995, para. 1)

210-day and 105-day cycles

An investigation of or reference to the duration periods of 105 days and 210 days has not been substantial, especially within academic Maya studies. It will be shown in this book, however, that these time periods may be more significant than previously thought. Following the 260-day Tzolkin sacred year, 105 days more are required to finish the 365-day Haab. Over a period of 2 years, the difference is 210 days (105 × 2).

According to Prudence M. Rice (2007) in *Maya Calendar Origins: Monuments, Mythistory and the Materialization of Time*, the 365-day Haab year is divided into a planting and growing period of 105 days (0.5 × 210) and a harvesting and devotional period of 260 days.

In other parts of the world, the 210-day period also holds significance. The Pawukon is a 210-day calendar that has its origins in the Hindu religion in Bali, Indonesia. The calendar consists of 10 different concurrent weeks of 1, 2, 3, 4, 5, 6, 7, 8, 9 and 10 days. In *Astronomies and Cultures in Early Medieval Europe*, Stephen C. McLuskey (1998) explains how the 210-day period was used by the ancient Hebrews when studying the lunar cycle:

> Over a full 19-year luni-solar cycle, the epact (the age of the moon on a specific date) will have increased by 11 days each year totalling 209 days, while seven intercalary months will have been inserted, reducing the epact by 30 days each time for a total of 210 days. (McLuskey, p. 81)

117-day cycle

A cycle of 117 days is another relatively obscure time duration the Maya have been known to study and which relates to other calendar periods (e.g. 117 × 7 = 819 days). In the article "On the Origin of the Different Mayan Calendars", Thomas Chanier (2015) writes:

> In Mesoamerican mythology, there are a set of 9 Gods called the Lords of the Night and a set of 13 Gods called the Lords of the Day. Each day is linked with 1 of the 13 Lords of the Day and 1 of the 9 Lords of the Night in a repeating 117-day cycle. (p. 3)

In her book *Star Gods of the Maya: Astronomy in Art, Folklore, and Calendars*, Susan Milbrath (1999) writes about the significance of the duration of 117 days with reference to the almanac calendar in the Dresden Codex, one of the few surviving codices from ancient Mesoamerica.

Christopher Powell also refers to this in his 1997 thesis, *A New View on Maya Astronomy*: "... the numbers 585 and 117 are also the number of days in the Venus and Mercury synodic periods used in an almanac on pages 30–33 of the Dresden Codex" (p. 29). A planet's synodic period is the time it takes to align in the same position relative to the sun when observed from the earth (University of Nebraska-Lincoln, n.d.). Mercury's exact synodic period is 115.88 days, approximately one fifth of the Venus synodic period of 583.92 days.

The following extract from a report in *Time* magazine by Jeffrey Kluger (2012) refers to what archaeologists believe is the oldest Maya mural ever found, which depicts the time duration of 117 days:

> The smallest timescales on the longer-range north wall are 117-day cycles, which coincide with the synodic period of Mercury—or the amount of time it takes for Earth and Mercury, when they are in a given position relative to each other, to return to that precise position as they move through their orbits. Other larger and more complex calculations suggest that the Mayans were trying to develop formulas to synchronize cycles of the moon, Mercury, Venus and Mars. These would then be assigned relevance in the Mayans' spiritual practices. (Kluger, 2012, para. 8)

Against a background of architectural design usually reflecting the philosophy of its creators, this research strives to revive the connection between the mathematics of the Maya calendar and their architecture. This work examines the Maya time frames within the context of geometry, mathematics and, in turn, the ratio and proportion of the Temple of Kukulkan. In the following chapters, I will show how these numerical patterns from the Maya calendar are linked to geometry, upon which I believe the temple design may be founded.

Chapter 2

The Defining Measurement

What mystery is this, unearthed, that stirs the soul from rest.
—Lindsay McAuley

It has been suggested that for a civilisation to flourish, a standardised system of weights and measures needs to be established. Historically around the world, as trade between neighbouring states developed, so too did the spread of a unified measurement system. Today, we have two primary systems, metric and imperial. There have been some attempts to resolve what system was used in pre-Columbian Mesoamerica.

Research was conducted by Patricia J. O'Brien and Hanne D. Christiansen (1986). They examined a number of Maya domestic buildings and concluded that a unit of measurement, which they called a Zapal, was in use. Its length was determined to be 147 mm (± 5 mm) and this was divided into 16 smaller units.

The unit of measurement I have found in the Temple of Kukulkan is different from this.

I am not disputing that 147 mm may have been a unit of measurement used by the Maya. My research is specific to this significant public temple. Considerable consultation between designers and architects would have been necessary before undertaking this project. I surmise there would have been a greater determination to achieve accuracy, more so than on a domestic building. In addition, the designers would have needed to maintain a consistent unit of measurement on such a large project to allow the builders to follow instructions from detailed plans. It would be virtually impossible without this fundamental unit to build a project of this size successfully. Nothing much has changed where the same applies today. To create a major structure like the Temple of Kukulkan, there would need to be a clear understanding between the architects and builders of the measurement system used on the site.

I believe my research accords with their philosophy as it is anchored to the Maya obsession with time, their calendar. This can be confirmed mathematically, primarily through the study of ratio and proportion.

Measuring the World

The world is created in the image of humankind, that is, the human-made world. Virtually everything we have built now and throughout history is an extension of the human body in some way. As is often the case in history, measurement systems have developed primarily using human anatomy as a reference. Those standards of human proportions have evolved to where, today, a relatively new profession has become an important part of our modern world—anthropometry.

The study of anthropometry takes into account human proportions, which are used to ensure design and construction is within the parameters of anatomy. Anthropometry makes use of statistical data in various industries such as design, clothing manufacture and ergonomics, as well as architecture. The distance to the steering wheel on your car is designed in accordance with a comfortable position for an average arm length. That proportional calculation is done by an anthropometrist. A teaspoon fits nicely into your hand. A doorknob is about the right height for an average-sized adult to reach easily. A chair is set at a reasonable height from the ground to sit at a table.

Throughout history, the proportions of the human body have set the size of the human-made physical world. Measurement is an extension of that principle. The basic units-of-length measurement from antiquity are also relative to aspects of anatomy. The ancient Romans used a unit of length named a "pace" based on the distance between two steps, which equalled about 1.5 m. Historically, the "foot", an obvious reference to human anatomy, may have been based on older measurements in Europe. Its length varied from country to country, over time falling somewhere between 250 mm and 335 mm long. It is now established as 304.8 mm.

Image 9: Egyptian cubit rod in the Liverpool World Museum (photograph by Dave Lightbody)

The cubit is a measurement that forms an integral part of this investigation. It has emerged as one of the most commonly used ancient dimensions, now superseded by metric and imperial. The word "cubit" is derived from Latin, *cubitum*, meaning elbow. Because there are various lengths attributed to the cubit, it does not produce a universal standard. It changed slightly over time as well as relative to geographic area.

There are two primary ways to determine its length. One is based upon the length of the forearm from the tip of the middle finger to the end of the elbow. The other method is to measure from the elbow to the base of the hand. These alternative descriptions complicate our capacity to determine an exact measure of the cubit, yet two variations emerge as a more widely accepted standard. They are known as the architectural or long cubit and the anthropological or short cubit. Archaeological evidence from Israel suggests that 525 mm and 450 mm constitute these lengths, respectively. To some scholars, the Egyptian cubit (Image 9) was the standard measure of length used during the early biblical period of around 600 BCE. Some writers assume the length of the Egyptian royal cubit, sometimes known as Ezekiel's cubit, to be the same as the architectural/long cubit, between 523 mm and 525 mm. The average or mean of these is 524 mm. The Egyptian translation for the cubit is *meh niswt*, and for the span it is *pedj-aa*. The span is exactly half a royal cubit, equalling somewhere between 261.5 mm and 262.5 mm, with 262 mm being the mean.

Chapter 2 : The Defining Measurement

One Step at a Time

Astronomy was revered by the Maya. Their civilisation was underpinned by a belief system that strived to function within an understanding of the movement of the cosmos. I propose that, as a harmonious expression of this philosophy, there was a relationship between astronomy, human anatomy and the measurement used at the Temple of Kukulkan. I am suggesting the Maya unit of measurement was based on the average height of the elevation of the human step when climbing a steep incline. This relationship contributed to determining the height of the steps.

It stands to reason that a temple elevated above the surrounding landscape implies its location is in the higher realms, the physical equivalent of being in an elevated state of consciousness. For the individual who aspires to understanding, achieving that understanding requires a journey, the ascension up the stairway. Walking up the stairway is a metaphor for the quest for higher knowledge. I sense this is one aspect of the reason why each step at the Temple of Kukulkan is approximately 262 mm high. It is compatible with the height of the foot while ascending an incline or stairway. But there is another remarkable value the Maya gave to this unit of length.

This height was also directly related to time and therefore the cosmos. Each step was assigned the value of the length of a day, the axis rotation of the earth. One day was the time duration that related directly to a physical measurement system. This interrelationship between anatomy, time and measurement produced an alignment between the Maya philosophy and their architectural environment. Every step up the ascending stairway was identified with the sunrise and sunset. As the foot was raised, the day began. As it reached the next step, the sun had set. It rises again ready for the next elevation.

A unit of measurement was more than just that. It encompassed the cycles of nature and of time, as well as human anatomy.

That great beacon of energy, the sun, brings about a new day and with it, a resurrection of life as darkness is overcome by the force of light. Translated into architecture, scaling the ascending stairway toward an elevated temple is comparable to following a rising pathway toward the ideal spiritual state. With each step, the cycles of nature become part of the journey. With each step, a new day is born. The transition between ignorance and knowledge corresponds with the sunrise and sunset. On the upward journey, each day is filled with the potential of ascension into the higher states of consciousness.

This observation is based on intuition and logic. The measurement height of the steps was an integral part of the Maya philosophy as it connects the temple architecture with time and the people of this remarkable mystical civilisation.

I believe the length used as a single unit of measurement in design and construction at the Temple of Kukulkan is 262 mm, which coincidentally is exactly half a royal cubit. Shortly, I draw links between this measurement and the ancient Mediterranean region.

This is where it gets really interesting and a little more abstract. I have determined that the height of each step on the Temple of Kukulkan not only represents one day but is a scale reference for the entire building. This was intentional and practical. The height of the steps is a key to understanding a very profound principle. It was an ingenious method of encoding the various Maya calendar lengths within architectural ratio and proportion.

I identified this key number, 262 mm, on some of the steps using 3-dimensional lidar scans as being the height of the riser and the length of the tread. The occasional one was out by 1–3 mm. Allowances should be made for the fact that this temple was built over 1500 years ago.

A more accurate way of determining the mean step height is by dividing the height to the platform, 23.9 m or approximately 23,900 mm, by the number of steps, 91.

$$23{,}900 \text{ mm} \div 91 = 262.6 \text{ mm} \approx 262 \text{ mm}$$

Usually 0.6 of a millimetre would be rounded up to the next complete unit, that is, 262.6 ≈ 263 mm. There is a reason for rounding it the opposite way. Throughout this book I will be suggesting there was a historical collaboration of intelligent minds from different civilisations. In light of that, I will be referring to the unit of measurement called the span, discussed earlier, which is half a royal cubit. The span equals somewhere

Chapter 2 : The Defining Measurement

between 261.5 mm and 262.5 mm. The mean of these two figures is 262 mm. I am suggesting that 262 mm was the intended height of the steps (0.5 of a millimetre is about the width of a line drawn with a ballpoint pen). Therefore, I am also proposing that the span, exactly half the length of a royal cubit, equals one day.

The most provable "intended" height to the platform by the original designers would therefore have been 23.842 m as opposed to 23.9 m, a variation of only 58 mm or 0.2%.

$$91 \text{ steps} \times 262 \text{ mm} = 23{,}842 \text{ mm} = 23.842 \text{ m}$$

The intended height of each step, 262 mm, will be the basis of all calculations in the following chapters.

Image 10: The base of the west-facing stairway

Standing at the base of the Temple of Kukulkan at Chichen Itza (Image 10), I had a strange feeling, as mentioned in the Preface. What was my connection here beneath the facade of stone and rock? Had I lost the plot, or had I found it? Was I heading down the rabbit hole of my own making? No, this is not fantasy. I am constantly reminded of its mathematical credibility. My brain had been rewired to receive this. Over the previous 25 years, an interest in sacred geometry had slowly opened doors to ways of receiving information from an unknown source, of perceiving patterns within mathematics, geometry and astronomy. I was preoccupied with studying the relationships between these disciplines almost to the point of obsession. The natural progression from this was to architecture. Perhaps this was an initiation of some kind. I had earned my way through this portal by means of hard work and focus. Getting to this point was a slow and sometimes tedious pathway full of conflict. Now, it feels as though the summit is in sight. The key to the mathematical proof is right there, in front of me. It was intelligently encoded in the height of the steps.

My intuitive insight is this:

The designers of the Temple of Kukulkan used a measurement length of 262 mm to represent one day, or, in the Mayan language, one k'in. The entire structure is governed by this scale measurement. Using ratio and proportion, this method allowed various calendar durations to be encoded within the different measurement lengths of the whole building.

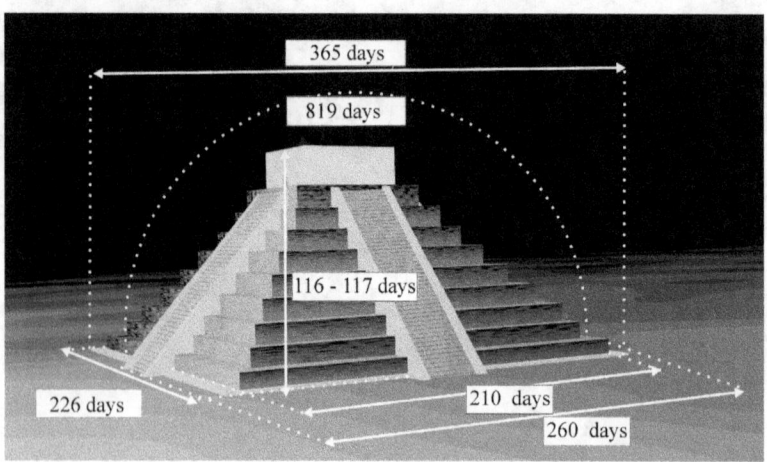

Diagram 2: The Temple of Kukulkan showing relative day-length dimensions

Diagram 2 gives you a direction and an outcome of what my research in the following chapters endeavours to prove mathematically. With the identification of the unit of measure used in the design representing one day, the Maya calendar durations can be calculated with less than 0.5% error or with 99.5% accuracy. Table A6 in the Appendix provides a summary, which indicates the level of accuracy. A more detailed mathematical analysis is provided in Tables A1 to A5.

Chapter 2 : The Defining Measurement

Image 11: The height of each step at Kukulkan

Image 12: Encoded within the architecture of the Temple of Kukulkan are the fluid cycles of time

One step = 262 mm; therefore, 262 mm = one day

The ancient designers used the axis rotation of the earth, equal to one day, as a reference for measurement. With this comprehension, understanding the mystical world of the Maya increases significantly. This technique of converting a physical length to a time duration allowed the designer to communicate their comprehension of humanity's part in the cosmos. It was there as a reminder for all members of this unique civilisation, who long ago understood this principle. For those who stood in front of the Temple of Kukulkan, the architecture was so much more than a pyramid. They would have had a perception of the intent of the designers, who encoded the fluid universal cycles of time in stone. Now, that information, which I hope to prove mathematically in this book, is available to you.

Metaphysical time and physical measurement are interchangeable.

Without an understanding of the use of the height of one step as the scale measurement of the entire temple, it is virtually impossible to ascertain whether any of the building's other dimensions are related mathematically. It is only with the knowledge that 262 mm equals one day that the calendar durations reveal themselves through mathematical analysis. Using this technique, it is possible to simultaneously encode several calendar durations illustrated within various ratios and proportions. This can be confirmed by measuring the temple in metres and then doing the conversion to days. The result is then correlated against time periods from the Maya calendar for comparison, as shown in Table 1 on the following page.

Chapter 2 : The Defining Measurement

Table 1: Temple of Kukulkan dimensions converted from metres to days

Reference	Description	Length (metres)	Conversion (millimetres)	Days
1. Primary measurements				
A1	Hypothetical circle circumference	214.578	214,578/262	**819**
A2	Hypothetical circle diameter	68.3	68,300/262	260.7 ≈ **260**
B	Height of step (average)	.262	262/262	**1**
C	Overall width (base of stringer to opposite stringer)	67.6	67,600/262	**258**
D	Diagonal of square based on C	95.6	95,600/262	364.9 ≈ **365**
E	Base of pyramid (side lengths)	55.6 55.7 55.1 55.2	55,600/262 55,700/262 55,100/262 55,200/262	212.2 ≈ **210** 212.6 ≈ **210** 210.3 ≈ **210** 210.7 ≈ **210**
F	Overall height	30.4	30,400/262	116.0 ≈ **117**
G	Height to platform	23.9	23,900/262	91.2 ≈ **91**
H	Stairway stringer length	34.3	34,300/262	130.9 ≈ 0.5 × **260**
I	Edge length of pyramid	30.4	30,400/262	116.0 ≈ **117**
2. Additional measurements				
J	Base of steps to opposite side	66.9	66,900/262	255.3
K	Stone border (side length)	59.2	59,200/262	226.0
L	Elevated platform (side)	19.9	19,900/262	76.0
M1	Elevated temple (height)	6.5	6,500/262	24.8
M2	Elevated temple (width)	15.1	15,100/262	57.6
N	Stairway width	8.53	8,530/262	32.6
O	Stairway width including stringer	11.9	11,900/262	45.4

DECODING THE LOST WORLD OF THE MAYA

| P | Angle of pyramid | 49.6°–50.8° | – | – |

Note. Measurements are as per independent examination of CyArk 3-dimensional lidar scans; see site reference map in Diagram 3.

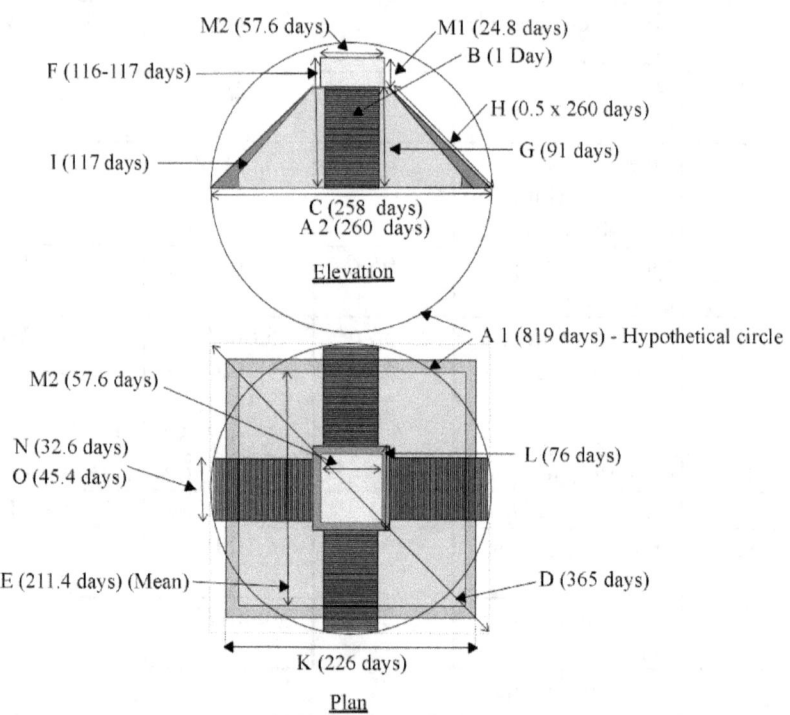

Site Reference Map - Temple of Kukulkan

Diagram 3: Temple of Kukulkan site reference map

This research provides evidence that suggests the 365-day Haab, the 260-day Tzolkin and other lesser known durations are purposely represented in the physical dimensions of the temple. I believe this mathematical information will stand up to scientific critique and be seen as empirical evidence.

For the average person to climb a stairway safely and without too much difficulty, the height of the tread and riser usually equals approximately 175 mm. This has become the standard height in construction in Australia. Making your way up the 91 steps on the temple, each of which is 262 mm high, forces the leg muscles to extend excessively. It is a considerable physical feat to make it to the top. Having no handrails adds another strain and has caused a few accidents for tourists who have made the attempt; several people have died on the climb. As a result, the temple is now closed off to the public.

This height of 262 mm is not an arbitrary measurement plucked out of the sky for no reason. It relates to anatomy in the lifting of a foot during the accent of an incline, as already mentioned. As well, it has some interesting parallels with a measurement used across the Atlantic Ocean more than 2000 years ago:

$$1 \text{ royal cubit} = 524 \text{ mm} = 2 \times 262 \text{ mm}$$
$$1 \text{ span} = \tfrac{1}{2} \text{ royal cubit} = 262 \text{ mm}$$
$$1 \text{ step} = 1 \text{ span}$$
$$2 \text{ steps} = 1 \text{ royal cubit}$$

Half a royal cubit is equal to a measurement length known as a span. A span of 262 mm is equal to the height of each step on the Temple of Kukulkan. Therefore, one step equals one span.

Could it be that by some stroke of luck the designers of the Chichen Itza pyramid accidentally, out of the blue and by some strange coincidence, just happened to start using the identical standard length also used in the Mediterranean region a couple of thousand years ago? I need to address this question because people have asked me to consider the possibility. That is, could two civilisations, although separated by a vast ocean, come up with an identical unit of measurement, given they were both knowledgeable about astronomy?

Firstly, this research is not just about astronomy. It is more about mathematics. It is more about a unit of measurement. The length from fingertip to elbow being identical in two distinct cultures is possible yet highly unlikely. In the context of this overall investigation, that should become clear as you read on. It becomes far less ambiguous as we study the geometry of the temple.

Apart from the fact it is a pyramid, nothing similar to this design exists in the Mediterranean region or anywhere else in the world for that matter. It is unique. It is an enigma.

One step equals one span. Two steps equal one cubit.

Sometime between 400 CE and 800 CE, Chichen Itza on the Yucatán Peninsula in Mexico was built. It is a long way from Israel and Egypt. The vast Atlantic Ocean separates Central America from the Middle East by about 12,000 kilometres. The cubit was used on the Temple of Solomon in Israel. It is far too coincidental that this same standard was also developed by the Maya and used as a measurement in a Maya temple. I suspect there was a collaboration of some kind.

This virtually identical measurement and the collaboration theory led me down another rabbit hole full of mystery and intrigue. I became interested in how this measure came about. It seemed more than a coincidence. As I investigated the measurement further, it became like a candle on a pathway lighting a winding staircase that led me back through ancient history. This pathway was mentally precarious and confusing. Regardless, I followed where it led.

As a general summary, 262 mm has the following qualities:

- It is the single unit of measurement used at the Temple of Kukulkan.
- It is based on the height of a human step while ascending an incline.
- It represents one day, the axis rotation of the earth.
- It provides a means to understand how calendar day-lengths are encoded in the architecture of the Temple of Kukulkan (research on other areas of the Chichen Itza site is not included in this examination).
- It is identical to a measurement used in the Mediterranean region thousands of years ago.

The Lost Tribe Pathway

Alternative theories surround the mysterious Temple of Kukulkan on the Yucatán Peninsula in Mexico and, indeed, much of Mesoamerican history in general. In this book, I draw plausible relationship links between this pyramid and the Mediterranean region. However, cultural diffusion is not a popular term in academia. I might step on a few toes here unintentionally. Suggesting the Maya were influenced by foreigners implies that they were not able to develop their own sciences without outside influence. I am saying there was a cultural collaboration. Yet, I am not the first to suggest ancient links between this civilisation and those from across the Atlantic Ocean.

Augustus Le Plongeon, a surveyor who lived and worked at Chichen Itza around 1873, was convinced that the symbols of Freemasonry could be traced to the ancient Maya. He believed this ancient knowledge had travelled to Egypt by way of Atlantis. His 1896 self-published book, *Queen M'oo and the Egyptian Sphinx*, contained many controversial views that were not given credibility by his contemporaries and were later disproven ("Augustus Le Plongeon," 2020).

In 1644, a Portuguese traveller and Marrano Sephardic Jew named Antonio de Montezinos convinced Menasseh Ben Israel, a rabbi of Amsterdam, that he had found one of the Ten Lost Tribes of Israel living in the jungles of Ecuador ("Antonio de Montezinos," 2020). Menasseh subsequently wrote a book, *The Hope of Israel* (Early English Books, n.d.). In it, he lends argument to the theory that the pre-Columbian native inhabitants of America are possibly descendants of the Ten Lost Tribes of Israel.

Nearly 200 years later in the early 19th century, that notion was again supported by Joseph Smith, the founder of the Mormon Church of Latter-day Saints. According to Smith, some of the indigenous people of the Americas were members of the lost tribes of Israel ("House of Joseph (LDS Church)," 2020). Mormons may learn of their tribal affiliation with Israelites. Mormon theology exists within the context of Judaism to an extent that goes beyond what most other Christian denominations claim. The faith incorporates many Old Testament ideas into its theology, and their beliefs often parallel those of Judaism and elements of Jewish culture. Members of the Latter-day Saints Church receive patriarchal blessings, which declare the recipient's lineage within one of the tribes of Israel, through either true bloodline or adoption. The Church teaches that if one is not a direct descendant of one of the Twelve Tribes of Israel, upon baptism he or she is adopted into one of the fold. Smith named the Mormon settlement he founded *Nauvoo*, which means in Hebrew "to be beautiful". The Church of Latter-day Saints has a centre in Israel where the study of Near Eastern history, culture and language is taught.

This historical Central American connection with ancient Israel stimulated my curiosity and perhaps my vivid imagination as well. It added a pretty wild and fanciful theory to this already mysterious story. I thought it would be interesting to stumble across evidence of the lost tribes. Well, it rapidly became more than intriguing. According to my research, I can state with some confidence that I have the strongest evidence to date of a foreign connection with Mesoamerica. All of this has arrived in my lap by coincidence and a little bit of providence … but from where and how, I have no idea.

Chapter 3

Measuring the Invisible

Philosophy is written in this grand book—I mean the universe—which stands continuously open to our gaze, but it cannot be understood unless one first learns to comprehend the language and interpret the characters in which it is written.
—Galileo Galilei, *Il Saggiatore* (1623)

It was not possible for me to come to a realisation about sensing I knew the mathematics of the pyramid, even though it was vague and abstract, then go back to Australia, make a cup of tea and think about something else. It was intuition that led to this, which may be called a point of no return. Sometimes I wanted to escape, but how could I run and hide from myself? I kept being lured back to complete the task. When there is the feeling of being communicated with from across the centuries, it cannot be ignored. With that, comes the very real questioning of one's own sanity.

The need to be right is very much a human condition. Surely, I cannot be wrong about this. If I can influence my readers to believe I am right, then I become even more right. It's a bit like religion. I had to work hard to prove to myself this was not completely fanciful or without foundation. Thankfully, my sense of being right is supported by evidence-based mathematics.

The need to prove the validity of a feeling became the next phase, to make tangible, the intangible, to make visible, the invisible. The process of mathematical interrogation begins. Here, in this chapter, I present that work, the equations to support the theory that the Maya integrated their calendar with architecture. The right-brain artistic, creative side needed to be balanced so the left-brain logical, analytical pathways could ignite, and they did. If you are not a mathematician, don't be alarmed; I am not either. If you are, I have employed a mathematician to check my calculations and to help write the formulas in the manner expected. This chapter documents the mathematical proof with which to support an intuitive hunch. It identifies patterns that emerge through finding number interconnectedness. These are then related back to the Maya calendar.

At first glance, art and mathematics seem to be worlds apart. Yet they are harmoniously connected through the process of recognising and appreciating patterns. A single number is like a single colour. As more colours are added, the art begins to take form. With the increase in numbers, complex patterns emerge. Numbers start communicating back to us in the same way art is able to move the viewer emotionally. We are taken to a place we have never been. When geometry is integrated, the canvas is enriched. Then, further still, add architecture. The depth of the artwork of mathematics becomes vibrant, permanent and alive.

It has been said that the human body produces an aura visible to those with a refined sensibility; so too, an aura of mathematics and geometry surrounds architecture.

The Number System

To acquire only a small grasp of astronomy, there is a need to have an understanding of mathematics. The Maya were one of the most mystical and mathematically oriented people from ancient history. They constructed a sophisticated number system, possibly more advanced than any other in the world at the same historical timeframe. They used a vigesimal or base 20 number system consisting of only three symbols: zero, represented as a shell shape; one, a dot; and five, a bar. Addition and subtraction was a relatively simple matter of adding up dots and bars. After the number 19, larger numbers were written in a vertical place-value format (Diagram 4).

Chapter 3 : Measuring the Invisible

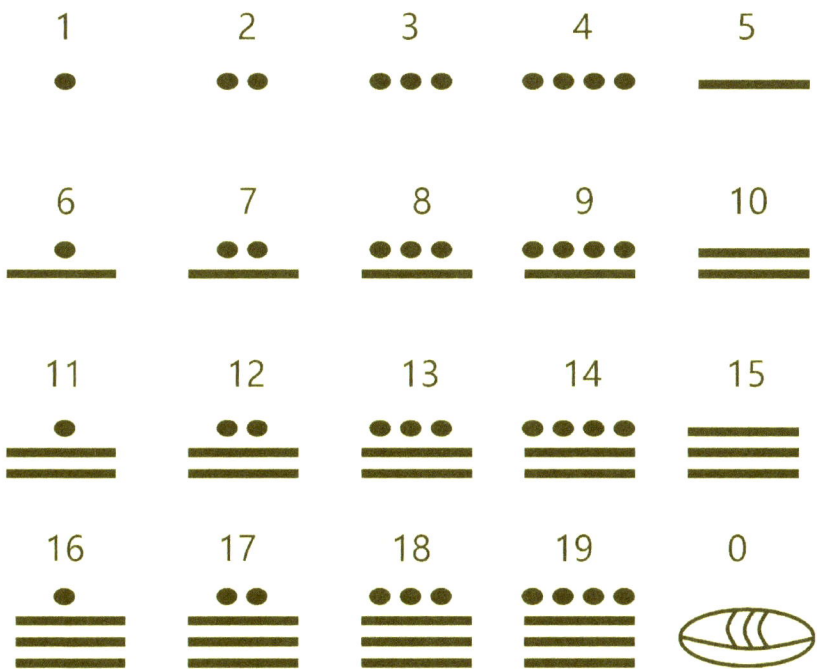

Diagram 4: The numerical Maya counting system

Archaeologists believe the Preclassic Maya and their neighbours had independently developed the concept of zero by as early as 36 BCE. There is evidence they worked with calculations up to hundreds of millions, and with dates so large it took several lines to illustrate them. They produced extremely accurate astronomical observations. We are yet to fully comprehend their scientific methods and techniques. We do know they were able to measure the length of the solar year to a far higher degree of accuracy than that used in Europe at the same time. Their calculations produced 365.24 days, compared to the modern value of 365.242198.

It is believed that due to geographical isolation, Maya and Mesoamerican mathematics had no influence from European and Asian numbering systems, but that remains to be seen. It also remains to be seen whether they had any concept of the use of a fraction. As already stated, archival records have been almost totally destroyed.

The Golden Ratio

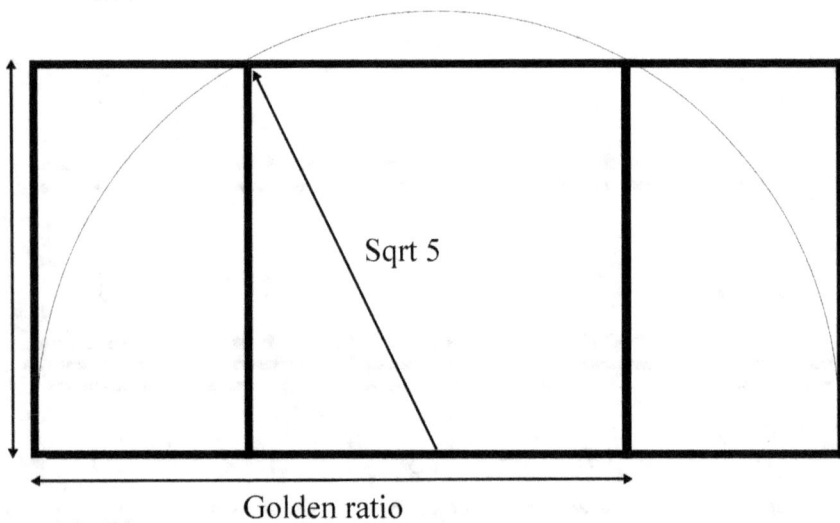

Diagram 5: The golden ratio 1.618

The golden ratio is claimed to have held a special fascination for humans for at least 2500 years. In mathematics, it is described as follows: two quantities are in the golden ratio if their ratio is the same as the ratio of their sum to the larger of the two quantities. That is a mouthful. In art, it is said to hold significant aesthetic qualities of harmony in terms of visual ratio and proportion (Diagram 5).

Generally, with any reference to the golden ratio from ancient history, the Maya civilisation is conspicuous by its absence. The ratio's development is usually attributed to the Egyptians and the Greeks, with the work of famous mathematicians such as Pythagoras and Euclid. However, researchers have recognised that the Maya designers had an understanding of the square roots of 2, 3 and 5, as well as the pi ratio. Peter Stewart, an archaeologist, presented a theory on Maya geometry in his book, *The Spiritual Science of the Stars* (Stewart, 2007). He found that modern shamans use standard geometric proportions in domestic buildings based on the square roots of 2, 3, 4 and 5, along with the golden ratio, phi. Research by Dr Christopher Powell (2010) in *The Shapes of*

Chapter 3 : Measuring the Invisible

Sacred Space documented that art panels at Palenque in Mexico reflect these geometric proportions.

My research seeks to extend our understanding of the significance to the Maya of both pi and phi and the use of the square roots of 2, 3 and 5. Using the pi ratio, square root formulas and geometry, I hope to prove the architects had complete knowledge of these calculations and successfully applied these methods to the design of the Temple of Kukulkan. In addition, I believe the Maya calendar has its roots in geometry; therefore, calendrical periods could be incorporated architecturally with the use of ratio and proportion. This could be achieved essentially by using a single unit of measurement commensurate with, and translatable to, one day. Assuming the Maya had an understanding of fractions, it is proposed in this research that they rounded off the numbers in the interests of practicality while maintaining a level of considerable accuracy.

The following are some examples of how the Maya calendar cycles are interconnected using mathematics. This also relates to the time-scale durations mentioned in this work. I will be referring to the most common Maya time periods of 260 and 365 days (the Tzolkin and the Haab, respectively), as well as lesser known durations such as the cycles of 819, 117 and 210 days. It will be shown here that the key dimensions of the pyramid can be linked to the 819-day period using the values of pi (3.14159…), the square roots of 2, 3 and 5, and the golden ratio, phi (1.618).

Using the 819-day duration designated as the circumference of a circle (measurement A1 in Table 1), it is possible to calculate several other calendar cycles with relative ease.

For example:

$819 \div \pi = 260.7 \approx$ **260** days

$819 \div \sqrt{5} \div \sqrt{2} = 259 \approx$ **260** days

$819 \div \sqrt{5} = 366.3 \approx$ **365** days

$819 \div \pi \div \sqrt{5} = 116.6 \approx$ **117** days

$819 \div \sqrt{5} \div \sqrt{3} = 211.5 \approx$ **210** days

$819 \div \pi \div 2 \times 1.618 = 210.9 \approx$ **210** days

Geometry relates to most Maya calendar cycles mathematically. It follows that this same geometry could be used as a design format for architecture. The calendar cycles are therefore accurately reproduced automatically using ratio and proportion.

Making the Invisible, Visible

The 819-Day and 260-Day Cycles

I propose that the 819-day calendar cycle was the primary base measurement for design and construction, represented geometrically in the circumference of a circle. From this circle shorter timeframes can be derived as shown in the previous section. This research suggests not only that the Maya calendar has a direct relationship to geometry but also that this geometry was used as the basis for the architectural design plan followed in the construction of the Temple of Kukulkan.

To follow the process, it is important to understand that a physical measurement must be converted to days. This is a relatively easy mathematical calculation. The scale measurement of 262 mm, the height of each step tread, is the basis of all calculations.

To convert from metres to days, divide by 0.262 m, for example:

$$10 \text{ m} \div 0.262 \text{ m} = 38.17 \text{ days}$$

To convert from days to metres, multiply by 0.262 m, for example:

$$100 \text{ days} \times 0.262 \text{ m} = 26.2 \text{ m}$$

The intention now is to show the linkage between the Temple of Kukulkan and the Maya calendar cycles by first identifying diagrammatically the mathematical connection between the 819-day and the 260-day calendar durations. This is done by overlaying the temple design plan within a circle. To see the relationship, I have compared the physical measurements in metres, as demonstrated in Diagram 6 on the following page.

Chapter 3 : Measuring the Invisible

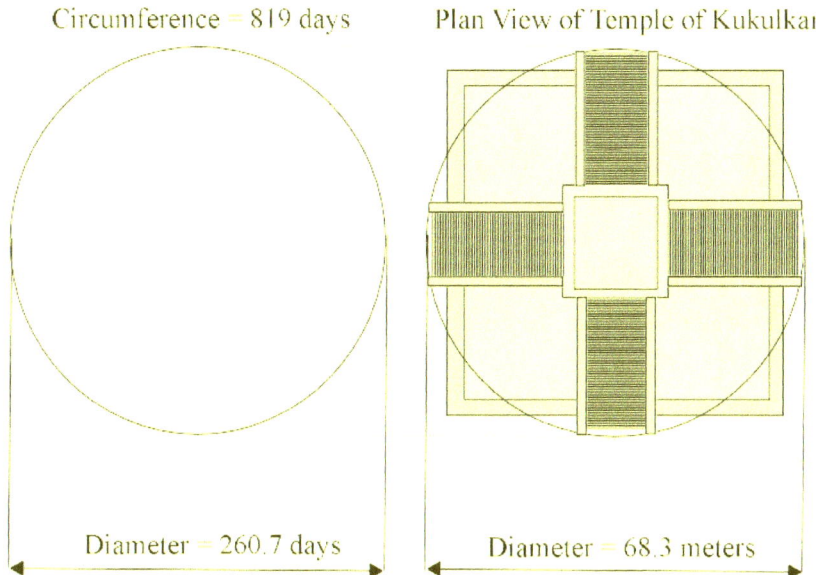

Diagram 6: *The comparative relationship between a circle and the plan of the Temple of Kukulkan*

The duration of 260 days converted to metres using the scale measurement of the height of the steps (262 mm) is equal to 68.1 m (260 × 0.262 m = 68.1 m).

If the architects intended the 260-day Tzolkin to be represented using the method of one day equalling 262 mm, then there should be evidence of a 68.1-m length somewhere in the design. There is, almost. It is in the overall width of the Temple of Kukulkan from the base of one set of stair stringers to the opposite side. How close is 68.1 m to the actual width of the temple? The comparative measurements are almost perfect (Diagram 7). However, almost is not good enough … perfect is.

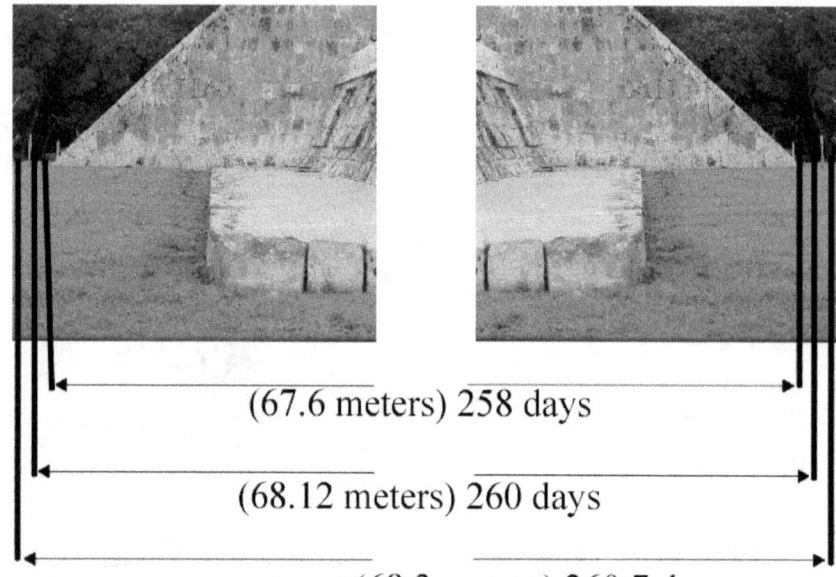

Diagram 7: The distance between the east and west stair stringers

The variation between the temple width and the hypothetical circle diameter is 700 mm, as shown using the following figures from Table 1:

Metres Circumference of circle (A1) = 214.578 metres

Diameter of circle (A2) = 68.3 metres

Width of Kukulkan (C) = 67.6 metres

Variation = 0.7 m or 700 mm

Days Circumference of circle (A1) = 819 days

Diameter of circle (A2) = 260.7 days

Width of Kukulkan (C) = 258.0 days

Variation = 2.7 days

Something is wrong. The measurements are out by almost three days if a circle of 819 days is used as a gauge, which produces a diameter of 260.7 days. If the centre point of the hypothetical circle was used as a reference, that would be 1.35 days either side, or 350 mm in the metric scale.

Chapter 3 : Measuring the Invisible

The Maya were perfectionists and so am I. It is more than a coincidence to be so close and yet not quite accurate. I presume they did not have a calculator like the one I have. They thought differently and had an alternative set of calculation methods at their disposal. Perhaps I am too determined to make their measurements fit perfectly into the dynamics of geometry using my modern tools and perspective. I need to introduce some flexibility into my theory because I am analysing the work of mathematicians and designers who lived almost 2000 years ago. My conceptual view requires a little realignment.

I have searched for a reason as to why the temple width was not exactly 260 days, finding that three factors need to be considered: (a) practicality in relation to building construction, (b) the Maya's understanding of the value of pi, and (c) the constraints of working within a circle.

In light of the overall width of the temple being so close to the calendar period of 260 days, I propose the following.

Firstly, being practical, it can be assumed the architects rounded 260.7 days down to 260 days, as 0.7 of a day would be difficult to negotiate in construction.

Secondly, their method of calculating the relationship of a circle's circumference to its diameter could have been slightly different from our contemporary understanding of producing pi. Today it is calculated as 3.14 … with infinite numbers after the decimal point. The ancient Egyptians estimated pi to be 3.16. Perhaps, 2000 years ago, the Maya calculated the ratio of the circumference of a circle to its diameter and that result came somewhere in between, at 3.15:

$$819 \div \pi = 260.7$$

$$819 \div 3.15 = 260 \text{ days}$$

But the temple width of 258 days is still short of the desired result by 2 days or 524 mm. How annoying!

The final factor that needs to be considered is working within a circle as a design feature. The measurement from the base of the step stringers to the opposite side is 67.6 m, which equals 258 days (67.6 ÷ 0.262 = 258 days). Where the step stringers end, they fall short of the hypothetical circle diameter (now 68.1 m or 260 days). But they would need to in order to fit within the curved boundaries. The variation of 2 days is plausible when considering that the arc of the circle would obviously extend out further than the end of the stringers, as shown in Diagram 8. In my view, this accounts for the discrepancy of one day either side of the temple.

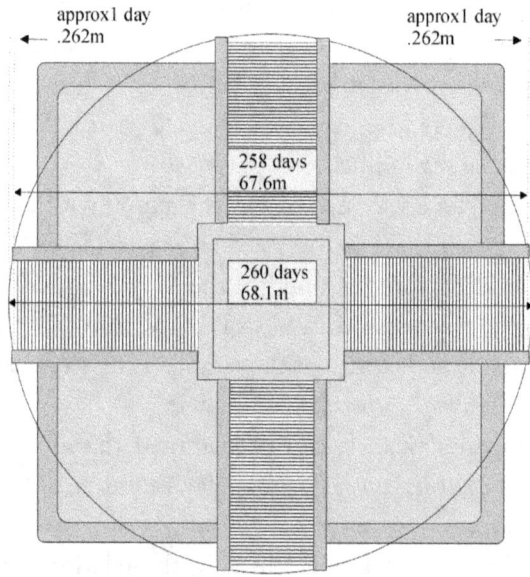

Diagram 8: Plan view of temple showing 262 mm or one day either side

In view of these factors, I propose the designers intentionally quantified the circumference of the hypothetical circle to equal 819 days, meaning the diameter of the circle would equal approximately 260 days. It is also possible they calculated the width of the temple using square roots as an alternative to pi, given that we are not certain they knew about decimal fractions. Knowledge of the use of square roots by the Maya is supported by the research of archaeologists Peter Stewart (2007) and Dr Christopher Powell (2010), as stated earlier. The square roots of 5 and 2 may have been used to determine the relationship of 819 days to 260 days:

$$819 \div \sqrt{5} \div \sqrt{2} = 258.99 \approx 259 \text{ days}$$

All things considered, the decimal variations, when the temple is recalculated using metres, become inconsequential provided there is less than 1% error. Decimal fractions, although necessary for estimating, can be more of an impediment to understanding the most likely intent of the designers if one does not introduce some degree of flexibility.

Factoring in all or any one of the previous considerations, it is highly probable that 260 days was the intended width of the temple to represent the diameter of the hypothetical circle. However, the actual width of the temple equals 258 days. Apart from the practicality of working within a circle, there may also be a scientific or cultural reason for this discrepancy of 2 days.

A resolution may be found in the night sky, with another perspective emerging through the study of astronomy. This concerns the planet Venus and the significance of 258 days within its observable orbital characteristics. The duration of Venus in the night sky is 258 days visible as the morning star. It periodically disappears from view because of its orbit of the sun in relation to that of the earth. It then reappears later as the evening star, visible once again for 258 days. The sun's blinding light obscures visibility because Venus is closer to the sun than Earth is. The planet Venus attracted considerable observational attention from the Maya, so 258 days would have been an essential time measurement within the Maya records of astronomy, which have now mostly vanished.

According to *Astronomy in the Ancient World* (McLeod, 2016):

> Another possibility has to do with an object we know had enormous significance in Maya culture and its predecessors: the planet Venus. The appearance of Venus as "morning star" is roughly 260 days (from its first appearance as morning star to its disappearance until its return as evening star). However, this is not exact, as Venus is visible as the morning star for 258 days, … (p. 26)

The validity of 258 days as an observable planetary event serves to significantly rectify the ambiguity of the reason for the two missing days, one day either side of the temple. It is a credible argument that the temple width would have been intentionally designed to represent a characteristic of Venus with the overall design being contained within the hypothetical circle.

The significance of 258 days has been written about by several authors. Chris Kasparis (2011) writes in his book, *2012—The Great Shift*:

> The 260 day Tzolkin is roughly 9 moon cycles, which incidentally also corresponds to the 9 month human gestation period! It is characterised by a number from 1 to 13 and by 20 day signs symbolised by hieroglyphs which have mythic themes and are also used as divinatory tools to forecast astronomical and astrological cycles. It was intimately linked to the appearance of Venus as the "morning star" and the "evening star" every 258 days and co-relates to planting and harvesting cycles, as well as planetary influences. (p. 33)

The design of the Temple of Kukulkan most likely represents the Venus cycle of 258 days in its width. The temple as a whole sits within the hypothetical circle representing the Tzolkin of 260 days as the diameter and the calendar cycle of 819 days as the circumference. This stands as the first of many examples of mathematical evidence to suggest it was intentional to make the width of the entire temple a particular size relative to the height of the steps.

The formula for calculating a segment of a circle (chord length) provides further credibility that a circle with a diameter of 260 days was likely used as a primary design feature, albeit invisible. The width of the steps (measurement N in Table 1) is 32.6 days, which is almost perfectly equal to the chord length (Diagram 9).

Radius: 130 days
Chord length: 32.6 days (width of steps)
Height: 1.02 days
Angle: 14.36°

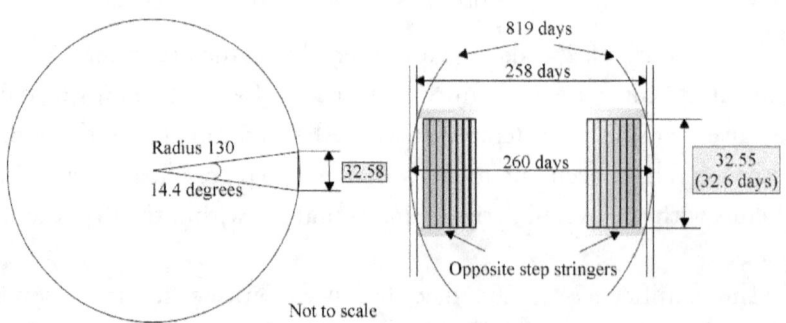

Diagram 9: The comparative length of a chord determining the width of the steps

Chapter 3 : Measuring the Invisible

$$c = 2r\sin\left(\frac{\theta}{2}\right)$$
$$= 2 \times 130 \times \sin\left(\frac{14.4}{2}\right)$$
$$\sin(7.2) \times 2 \times 130 = 32.58 \ (2 \text{ dec. pl.}) \approx 32.6$$

According to one of my maths tutors, Diagram 10 using the Pythagorean theorem is of particular interest. It offers substantial evidence to support the use of a circle as the basis for the design. The width of the steps fits this model accurately.

The irony is, should the width of the temple equal 260 days exactly, this would provide less compelling evidence of the 819-day circle being the foundation design feature.

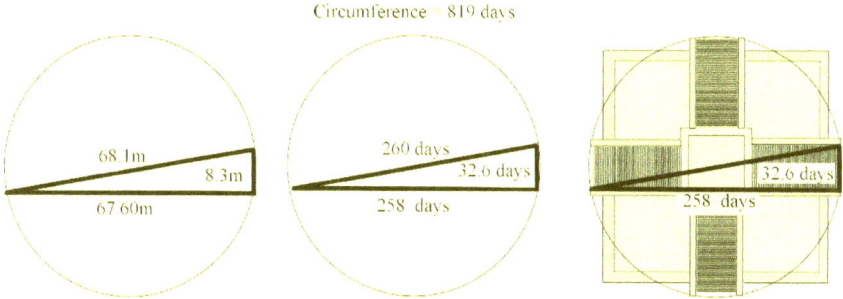

Diagram 10: Using the Pythagorean theorem, the hypotenuse equals 260 days

$$\text{hypotenuse} = \sqrt{258^2 + 32.6^2}$$
$$\text{hypotenuse} = 260.05 \approx 260 \text{ days}$$
$$\text{Width of steps} = 8.53 \text{ m } (8.53 \div 0.262) = 32.6 \text{ days}$$

These calculations of the temple ratios raise the question: Did the Maya know about complex mathematical concepts such as trigonometry, the Pythagorean theorem, pi ratio to the value of 3.15 and how to calculate the segment of a circle thousands of years ago?

The various lengths and heights of the Temple of Kukulkan are multiples of one-day lengths (one k'in). By counting the number of divisions equalling 262 mm within any overall length, a specific result in days can be derived. It has been shown here that an almost perfect ratio of 1:260 exists between the height of each step and the diameter of the hypothetical circle. With the width of the temple, the ratio is 1:258, which indicates a highly probable connection to the planet Venus.

As the ratio of the k'in is to the Tzolkin, so is the height of the steps to the hypothetical circle diameter that determines the width of the Temple of Kukulkan.

The Maya were a barbaric lot, that is, according to my travel agent. This is the reputation they have out there in mainstream media. It is the gutter journalism that puts all the ugly stuff forward to get attention. Let us go straight to the dark side. "Pagan sacrifice" and "devil worshippers" apparently are better headlines than "spiritual mystics with a high degree of artistic sensibility". To me, it is incongruent for someone to be studying mathematics, architecture and astronomy one minute, which requires considerable intellect, then chopping heads off the next. However, a civilisation, a society, is made up of all personality types, and murder is not uncommon in any country on earth, including so-called developed ones. It is happening on every continent even as I write this. The other peculiar thing worth mentioning is that the Maya civilisation ended and nobody knows where they went. They just disappeared. The 7 million Maya who now live in Guatemala and the 30 million or so now living in the USA who claim Maya ancestry as their heritage would probably argue about the rumour that the Maya are extinct.

They were obsessed with accuracy. My analysis of the 3-dimensional scans of the Temple of Kukulkan revealed their precision: the construction plan for the base of the pyramid is accurate to within half a metre over 55 metres. My 3-dimensional lidar scan technician was surprised to see that the temple is virtually perfect as far as being level. It was built over 1600 years ago without laser levels or the modern apparatus we use today. That indicates the Maya were an advanced, intelligent community of gifted designers and engineers. Every day was significant to the ancient Maya. Each day had a name that guided them how to go about a particular day. They were fantastic artists, engineers and builders. I believe that capacity is embedded in the ancestral genes of every Maya alive today.

As already shown in this section, the 819-day cycle is represented in the circumference of a circle, with the 260-day cycle most likely represented as the diameter of that circle. The following sections continue the mathematical examination of other calendar periods: the 365-day, 117-day and 210-day cycles.

The Haab (365-Day Cycle)

I became interested to learn how long ago early astronomers recognised accurately the number of days it takes for the earth to revolve around the sun. Today, we know it takes 365.242 days. That is the number of revolutions of the earth on its axis in one orbit of the sun.

It seems Hipparchus, born in Turkey in 190 BCE, is given credit as one of the first to recognise this. Much of his research was thought to be derived from the Babylonians. He is also credited with being one of the first to predict eclipses ("Hipparchus," 2020). However, the Maya may have accurately predicted astronomical phenomena centuries ahead of that time. A 2011 book, *Astronomy in the Maya Codices* (Bricker & Bricker, 2011), details a series of impressive observations made by Maya astronomers.

Anthropologists Harvey and Victoria Bricker have conducted most of their work by translating complex hieroglyphics from four different Maya codices housed in Madrid, Paris, Mexico and Dresden. They found that the astronomical calendar dated to the 11th or 12th century accurately predicted a solar eclipse—the eclipse that occurred on 11 July 1991—to within a day. This date is centuries after the Maya civilisation ended.

Neatly ordered columns of carefully rendered hieroglyphic texts and numerals found in Xultún, Guatemala, dated to be in the Classic period (ranging from 250 to 900 CE), add up to 6704 years. The Maya were not content with small timeframes. The Maya may have been as advanced as any other civilisation in determining the axis rotation of the earth.

I did not invent the theory that the Maya purposely used astronomy or aspects of their calendar within the design of architecture. This theory has been around for some time. My work is an expansion of that arbitrary suggestion already mooted.

Diagram 11: One of the four stairways on the Temple of Kukulkan, each with 91 steps

As Diagram 11 shows, the Temple of Kukulkan has four stairways to the top platform, each with 91 steps. Because of this, the general assumption by most accounts is that the designers intended the observer to add the number of steps on the four stairways together to arrive at a figure representing one of their calendar time periods, the Haab. It is an elementary calculation:

$$91 \times 4 \text{ stairways} = 364$$

With the addition of the final step entering the temple, this would equal the duration of the 365-day year, the Haab. Albeit based on basic addition, this calculation is the most widely recognised and documented analysis that suggests the Maya intended the Temple of Kukulkan to represent aspects of their calendar system.

However, to prove the legitimacy of my observations, I take concrete analysis of this principle of integrating their calendar in architecture to a whole new level. The research presented here is rock-solid, evidence-based proof reliant on meticulous mathematical analysis of accurate 3-dimensional scans. It may be described better as obsessive-compulsive. This was a necessary process. Using calculations based on the scale measurement of

Chapter 3 : Measuring the Invisible

the height of the steps, this research extends an existing anecdotal theory significantly. However, this research is brand new because it is the first time, to my knowledge, a single unit of measurement has been identified and related mathematically to the Maya calendar. This includes the Haab, as well as several other known calendar durations. This was achieved and therefore only recognisable by identifying and understanding the unit of measure used during design and construction.

Diagram 12 shows how the diagonal of a square with a side equal to the length between the stairway stringers or the overall width of the temple, 258 days or 67.6 m, accurately calculates the Maya Haab of 365 days simply by using either the Pythagorean theorem or the square root of 2.

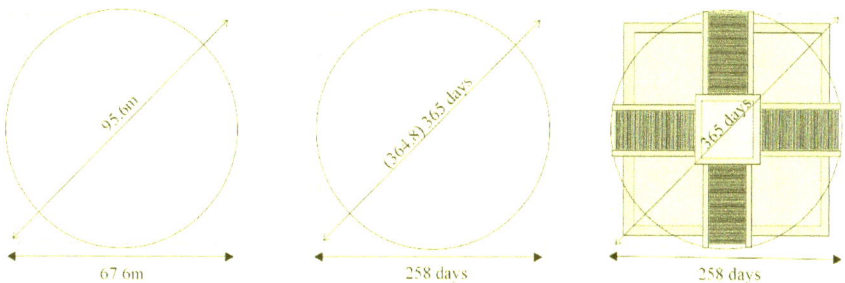

Diagram 12: Hypothetical diagonal length equal to the 365-day Haab

$$\text{hypotenuse} = \sqrt{67.6^2 + 67.6^2} = 95.6 \text{ m}$$

$$95.6 \text{ m} \div 0.262 = 364.9 \approx 365 \text{ days}$$

$$\text{(alternatively) } 67.6 \text{ m} \times \sqrt{2} = 95.6 \text{ m}$$

$$258 \times \sqrt{2} = 364.9 \approx 365 \text{ days}$$

This method of identifying the Haab adds weight to the general consensus already speculated by the process of adding the number of steps on each stairway together to achieve an accurate result of 365 days.

The 117-Day Cycle

Standing at the base of the temple, I entertained the notion that if the stairway extended all the way to the top, what secret measurement would that reveal? On the internet I found a multitude of measurements indicating the height of the pyramid from ground level, all of which seemed to be based on guesswork or on copying someone else's guesswork. I reverted to my CyArk 3-dimensional lidar scans for an accurate assessment. After doing the calculation, I hastened back to the internet to find out the significance of the result. The measurement produced by the scans gives a height of 30.4 m (measurement F in Table 1):

$$30.4 \text{ m} \div 0.262 = 116 \text{ days}$$

I scanned the internet for a Maya calendar measurement that was close to 116 days or a reference that was somewhere near it. Perhaps an archaeologist had found evidence of this number in a cave somewhere. It took a little time; however, I found one, which I referred to in Chapter 1. It was 117 days. This was one day off what I had hoped for.

It was one day too many as compared with my calculation of the height of the temple. This forced me to wonder what was wrong. So near and yet not perfect. Just as the width of the temple base was out by approximately one day either side, so was the height, by only 262 mm.

I had found a resolution previously, so again I searched for a possible explanation for the one-day variation.

Architectural drawings are designed to assist builders to follow a construction process. They show details of measurements, including plans and elevations. Invariably, when it comes to translating perfect design measurements from paper into bricks and mortar, or in this case stone, there is usually a discrepancy in real-world measurements. It is the same now as it was most likely a thousand years ago. This fact, together with encroaching rainforest vegetation and subsequent rectification of substrates, means allowances should be made during this analysis. Perhaps there was some subsidence over the last 1600 years. Therefore, this analysis has two parts, which I call "intended" and "actual".

Intended: implies the completed work would be a precise representation of the architectural drawings.

Actual: the final measurements that may not be exactly as the designer expected.

Chapter 3 : Measuring the Invisible

Reasonable judgement suggests what the intended measurement should be, based on a number of factors. In this context, there is evidence of 117 days being a Maya timeframe. We have already deciphered the 819-day duration and the 260-day Tzolkin being built into other dimensions. A reasonable conclusion would be the Maya would not stop there and would want to represent other calendar periods.

I suspect that the intended measure for the completed height of the entire pyramid would be the 117-day duration, which is equivalent to 30.654 m (117 × 0.262), a difference of only 254 mm from the actual height of 30.4 m. The builders got it right to within 262 mm, or one day, over the height of the entire building, a remarkable achievement in anyone's terms. It is a worthwhile exercise to locate 262 mm on a tape measure to see the relative size. If you happen to be standing next to the Temple of Kukulkan or anything (about) 30 m in height, then it can be recognised just how accurate the builders actually were.

The duration of 117 days has a mathematical relationship to the hypothetical circle of 819 days and can be calculated with relative ease:

$$819 \div \pi \div \sqrt{5} = 116.6 \approx 117 \text{ days}$$
$$260 \div \sqrt{5} = 116.3 \approx 117 \text{ days}$$

Diagram 13: The height to the top of the temple measured in days

In the context of this comparative examination and if I am to be scientific about it, I need to study actuals rather than hypotheticals. Another striking feature becomes evident simply by using the square root of 5 (= 2.236). The temple's height-to-width ratio almost exactly equals this measurement, which leads me to consider that 116 days, or 30.4 m, really was the intended height.

$$116 \times \sqrt{5} = 259.4 \approx 260 \text{ days}$$
$$116:260 = 1:2.24$$

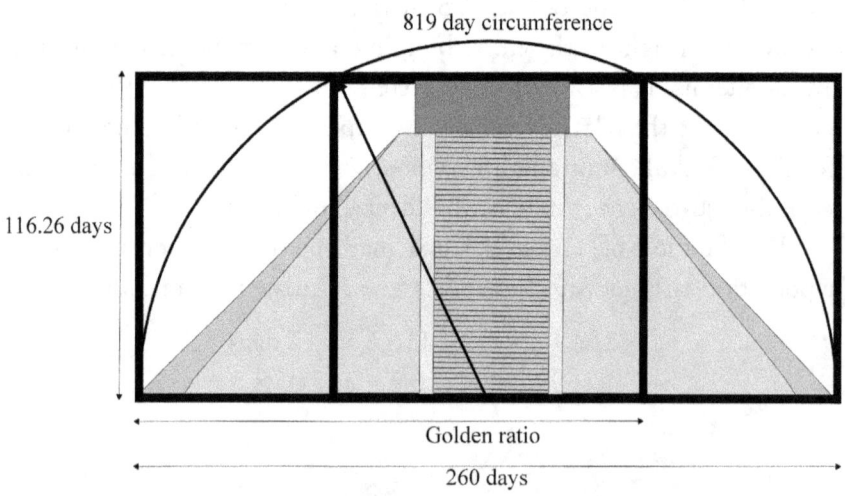

Diagram 14: The dimensions of the Temple of Kukulkan and its relationship to the golden ratio (1.618) and the $\sqrt{5}$ (2.236)

I have never seen the ratio of the height of the temple to its width documented using the square root of 5 before. Perhaps this is because it has never been measured from the perspective of using days as a unit of measure. It was worthwhile using the 3-dimensional lidar scans because this shows the designers were conscious of the square root of 5 number, as archaeologist Peter Stewart (2007) has already suggested. The golden ratio, 1.618, and the square root of 5, 2.236, are geometrically related (Diagram 14). This to me has significant credibility because of its simplicity and effectiveness in the use of mathematics and geometry to establish ratio.

If 116 days was the intended height, there are also some interesting parallels with astronomy. Mercury's synodic period is 115.88 days. This is almost identical to the height of the temple, being within 0.12 days. If the temple's width was intended to represent Venus, then conceivably Mercury may qualify as the height. A relationship to the Maya's dedication to observing the planets and thus incorporating some of their characteristics in the temple is also beginning to emerge (Diagram 15).

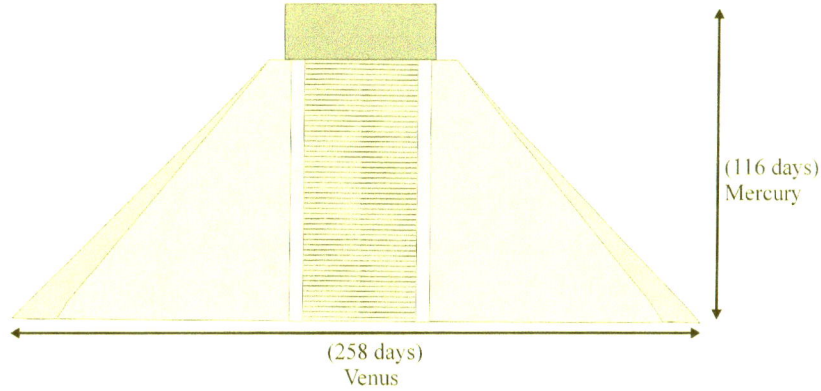

Diagram 15: The dimensions of the Temple of Kukulkan and its relationship to Venus and Mercury

Similarly, in Diagram 16, the 365-day Haab can be seen represented in the height of the temple within the circumference of a circle (116 days is a more accurate calculation of the 365-day Haab than if it were a 117-day height).

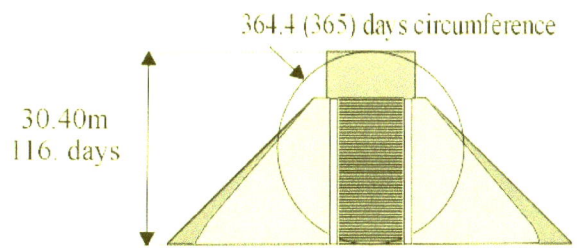

Diagram 16: The circumference is equal to the 365-day Haab

$$116 \times \pi = 364.4 \approx 365 \text{ days}$$

Summarising the calculations so far, the width of the Temple of Kukulkan is based on the calendar cycle of 260 days, with a secondary relationship to the 258-day cycle of Venus. The temple's height is based on the calendar cycle of 117 days, as well as Mercury's 116-day synodic period. The diagonal of the base is 365 days, equalling the Haab. All these calendar durations are based on an 819-day circumference. Evidence has emerged to suggest the original intent of the designers. Calendar durations, planetary observations and physical ratios are blended into one architectural design.

The 210-Day Cycle

According to the measurement results from the 3-dimensional lidar scans, the lengths of the four sides of the temple base are listed in Table 2. These vary a little between each other, yet are considerably more accurate than the internet's multitude of estimations, yielding on average 55.4 m. The Maya were able to achieve considerable accuracy, to within 0.6 m or 600 mm, over this distance.

Table 2 shows the conversion to days based on these measurements.

Table 2: Temple of Kukulkan pyramid base side lengths converted from metres to days

Base of pyramid	Side length (metres)	Conversion (millimetres)	No. of days
West face			
Left side	55.6	55,600/262	212.2 ≈ **210**
Right side	55.7	55,700/262	212.6 ≈ **210**
North face			
Left side	55.1	55,100/262	210.3 ≈ **210**
Right side	55.2	55,200/262	210.7 ≈ **210**

Chapter 3 : Measuring the Invisible

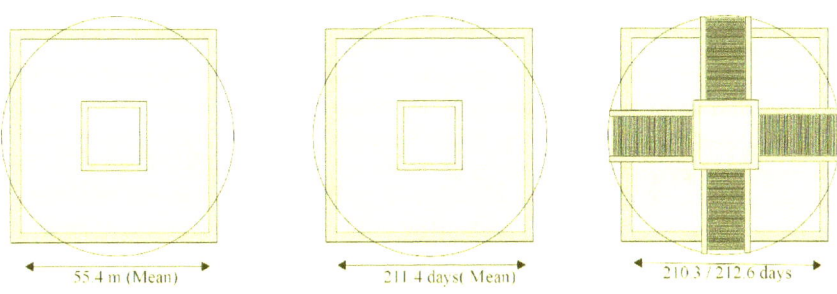

Diagram 17: The mean length of the base of the temple corresponds to the 210-day cycle

Here at the base, we have one of the most salient dimensions, the width of the main pyramid, indicating the time reference of 210 days. This time period is rarely documented, but we must remember the Maya astronomy records have been mostly destroyed. This length of time must have held some major significance to the Maya for it to be assigned to this primary dimension of the base of Kukulkan. The 210-day width of the pyramid is related to other dimensions in a number of ways, which demonstrates just how carefully planned the entire construction design was.

- Haab $\quad\quad\quad 365 \div \sqrt{3} = 210.7 \approx$ **210** days
- Tzolkin $\quad\quad 260 \times 0.5 \times 1.618 = 210.3 \approx$ **210** days
- hypothetical circle $\ 819 \div \sqrt{5} \div \sqrt{3} = 211.5 \approx$ **210** days
- golden ratio $\quad 819 \div \pi \times 0.5 \times 1.618 = 210.9 \approx$ **210** days

Stone Border Marker

Image 13: The stone border around the perimeter of the pyramid

At the base of the Temple of Kukulkan is what I call a stone border extending around the full perimeter of the building (Image 13). At first glance, this architectural addition seems to serve no purpose other than as a walking platform and could easily be overlooked as nothing more than ornamental. However, my analysis of its side-length measurements suggests it is meant as a crucial design feature. Unfortunately, I only had time to obtain one measure, which equalled 59.2 m. Converted to days, this equals 226 days. This is very close to the orbital characteristic of Venus. I believe the dimensions of the perimeter may have been designed to identify with this planet as well as having a relationship to other dimensions using the golden ratio. Modern science has determined the orbit of Venus to be 224.7 days, as compared with the 226-day actual measurement of the stone perimeter of the temple. This may be seen as an additional Venus relationship built into the temple, but lo and behold, there is that almost perfect, one-day variation again.

Diagram 18 shows the relationship between the stone border and the diagonal using the golden ratio, phi (1.618).

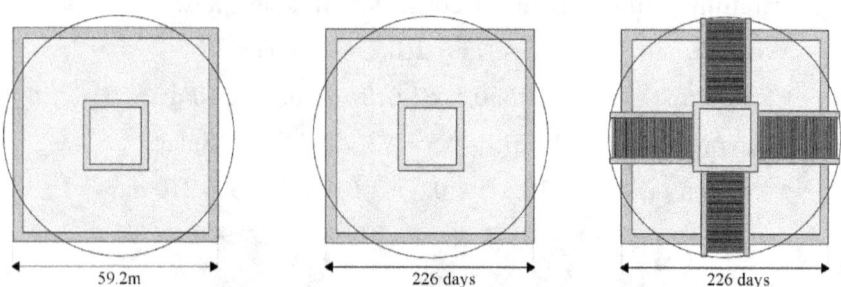

Diagram 18: The dimensions of the stone border

$$226 \times 1.618 = 365.7 \approx 365 \text{ days}$$

$$\text{Golden ratio: } 210 \div 1.618 = 129.8 \approx 130 \; (0.5 \times 260)$$

Venus was one of the most important planets in the night sky to the Maya. In the Dresden Codex, the Maya had an almanac displaying the full cycle of the Venus synodic period. In Chapter 4, this measurement length of the stone border opens up a completely different perspective, one that challenges our perception about who else may have been involved in the construction of the temple. The Temple of Kukulkan displays the golden ratio thereby increasing its harmonious aesthetic appeal (Diagram 19).

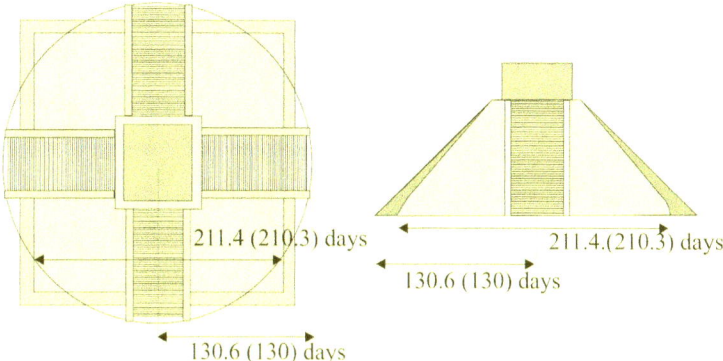

Diagram 19: The plan view relative to the elevation showing the golden ratio

In summary, I believe the results provide concrete mathematical evidence to support the theory that the design of the Temple of Kukulkan was intended to represent the Maya calendar cycles. There is clear mathematical proof of the existence of several timeframes represented through ratio and proportion. They are written in stone on the Temple of Kukulkan as a record from the past of an advanced civilisation whose mathematical and design capacity has been largely underestimated. The Maya's knowledge of geometry is rarely documented. Now, with this new information, I hope they may be recognised as scientifically more advanced than ever before.

Here are the measurements once again:
- Height of one step = 1 day
- Hypothetical circle circumference = 819 days
- Hypothetical circle diameter = 260 days
- Overall width of temple = 258 days (possibly representing Venus)
- Diagonal of square based on overall width = 365 days
- Height of temple = 117 days = 116 days (possibly representing Mercury)
- Length of pyramid base = 210 days
- Side of stone border = 226 days = 224.7 days (possibly representing Venus)

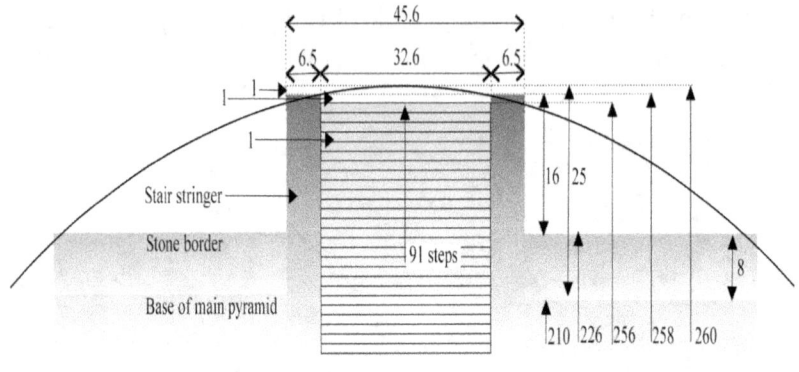

Diagram 20: Detail of proposed intended dimensions of the stairway area

Image 14: The temple on the elevated platform

Finally, on the temple which sits on the elevated platform, a sculptured face is set into one of three rectangles (Image 14). It is unknown who this represents with any degree of certainty. Because of lost records, any opinion would only be speculative. Perhaps it is meant to represent Kukulkan himself. I was more interested in the proportional measurements.

    I speculated that if the height of the steps were used as the scale measurement of the entire building, then this centrepiece should also hold a

Chapter 3 : Measuring the Invisible

reference to those same values. It does. The centre rectangle is 1.834 m wide. I did the conversion:

1.834 m ÷ 0.262 = 7 days

I see this as additional evidence and a confirmation that 7 days is also a significant timeframe to the Maya. The other two rectangle measurements are each approximately 2.09 m wide. This may be intended to represent a timeframe of 8 days (8 × 0.262 = 2.096 m); however, I cannot conclusively verify this until I have access again to the CyArk 3-dimensional lidar scans. Nor have I been able to determine the exact height of the rectangles with any degree of accuracy.

It is self-evident. The intention of the Maya designers is clear. The Temple of Kukulkan is the Maya calendar recorded in stone using the height of each step as a scale reference.

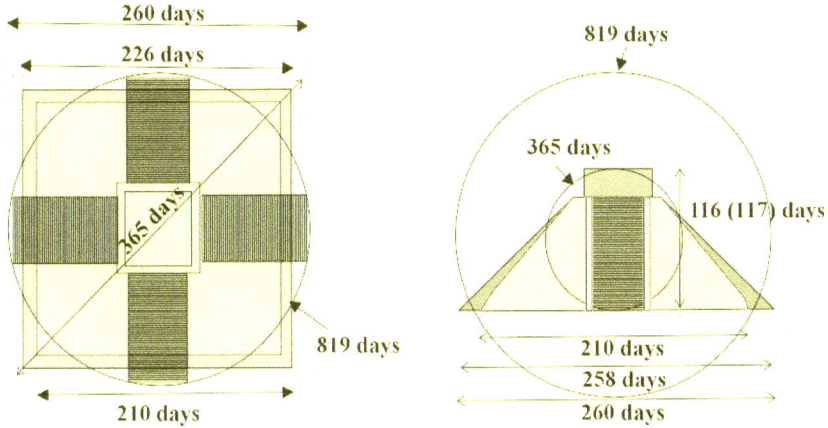

Diagram 21: Various day-length dimensions represented in the Temple of Kukulkan in plan and elevation views

Further examination of reasons for the extra one day either side of the temple between 258 days and 260 days, and in its height between 116 days and 117 days, is warranted. It seems to suggest this design characteristic may have been intentional, holding metaphysical, esoteric value. Imagine the Maya, who were gifted in their knowledge of astronomy, wanted to build an invisible aura around the temple. I believe this is within their creative conceptual ability. It appears to me they have made an attempt at doing this as one day rectifies most mathematical inconsistencies, bringing the structure into alignment with their calendar. Assigning the calendar values to the hypothetical circle creates an observation that, possibly, an invisible mathematical force field surrounds the physical structure of the temple contained within the hypothetical circle's boundaries. The hypothetical circle is not so hypothetical after all.

The Temple of Kukulkan harmonises with the intent of creating an architectural masterpiece congruent with their cultural belief systems as well as illustrating scientific observations from astronomy.

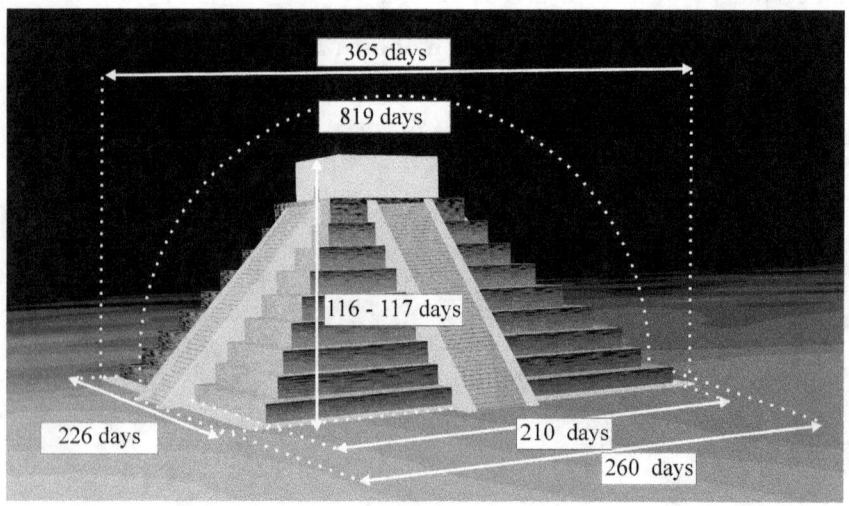

Diagram 22: The Temple of Kukulkan showing the relative day-lengths

Chapter 4

I Was Here

Before going any further, I had better apologise pre-emptively as I am about to upset somebody with the content in this chapter for sure. Going into this terrain is often fraught with conflict. However, I have to present my truth the way I see it. Having said sorry already to anyone who may choose to get their fur rubbed up the wrong way, I have transferred the problem of disposing of their issue back to them.

We all like to leave our mark. A strange aspect of human nature is the desire to let people who come after us know that we have been to a particular location. We scratch our name on a rock, in the bark of a tree, anything that records our presence. Some of us leave ink on a page and write books. Perhaps it is a primal way of marking our territory, or we just want to let people who come after us know where we went in our travels.

What an interesting way of leaving a record of presence: by incorporating a measurement system into architecture. Very clandestine and somewhat profound. Definitely indelible. That is what I suspect might have happened sometime in the ancient history of Mesoamerica. Ironically, that measurement used in Central America is identical to what was used in the Mediterranean region over 2000 years ago. What had me intrigued though is how it might have made its way across the Atlantic Ocean to Central America, or the New World, as it was once called.

It is conceivable that someone would attempt the journey across the Atlantic Ocean but, if they did, why bother leaving a unit of measurement as a permanent reminder of their presence? Did they see it of paramount importance to purposely leave a record of where they went for future generations, a secret encoded in architecture? Perhaps. It seems extreme, to say the least. In practical terms, a measurement system would be way down on the survival list, well after food and water. If it were a historical fact that this happened, then its value must have been deemed extremely high to be on the manifest of useful things to take on a long boat journey. The alternative is that there may have been a pre-planned voyage, one that could have consisted of numerous ships with cargo to last several months. There may have been an attempt to set up a complete infrastructure for a new beginning or to re-establish a civilisation. A measurement system would definitely then be on the list of essentials. Hypotheticals upon more hypotheticals.

I trawled the internet looking for a solution to how a measurement unit may have found its way to Central America. Not being a historian, I had a huge learning curve in front of me. If you are more knowledgeable than me with regard to the biblical period of history, feel free to correct me. My job as a professor at Harvard University will not be at risk as I am not likely ever to work there. However, I will do my best.

The nice thing about ancient history is that everyone can be completely wrong and also, terribly right. No one will ever know for certain.

Something caught my eye by accident while perusing the internet looking for possibilities. It was a sailing ship about to set out across the Atlantic Ocean. Called the *Phoenicia*, it was a 600 BCE Phoenician replica. The voyage was planned for September 2019. I recognised this event as providence at work behind the scenes. I knew I had to find the captain. I had to pull out every resource at my disposal and make sure the universe aligned. It was so integral to my story. It was the anchor that backed up the second part of this most remarkable journey. It linked directly to that measuring rod found in the ancient crypt, which I referred to in the introduction of this book. I just had to get on board that vessel one way or another. It was the most provable key to why the measurement on the temple was identical to that used in the ancient Mediterranean region.

The Hypothetical of the Ark, the Rod and the Boat

A couple of thousand years ago across the Atlantic, 12,000 kilometres from Chichen Itza, over one third of the planet away from the jungles of Guatemala, an event was taking place. It was in the biblical era at the time of King Solomon in the region we now call Israel. Construction on Solomon's Temple had just been completed (Image 15). The year was somewhere around the mid-10th century BCE. It is believed that the Temple of Solomon housed the Ark of the Covenant.

*Image 15: Artistic representation of Solomon's Temple, 10th century BCE (illumination by Jean Fouquet from a 15th century French edition of Flavius Josephus's **Antiquities of the Jews**)*

As the legend goes, the Ark contained three things: the two stone tablets of the Ten Commandments, Aaron's rod and a pot of edible substance known as manna. The Ten Commandments were delivered to Moses on

Mount Sinai. Aaron's rod was believed to be endowed with miraculous power used during the Plagues of Egypt that preceded the Exodus. An apocryphal Christian legend states that Aaron's rod was cut from the Tree of Knowledge.

However, instead of a walking stick with magical powers, I surmise Aaron's rod was more likely a measurement gauge used to establish uniformity of the length of the cubit. The Tabernacle, the Temple of Solomon, and many other structures are described in the Bible by cubit measures. Measurement was of paramount importance to people of the biblical era, including the Egyptians. By most accounts, the Ark of the Covenant was 2.5 cubits long by 1.5 cubits wide. A normal-sized walking stick might be too long to fit in it. A cubit measurement rod no longer than 524 mm would fit very nicely.

So, to make a short hypothetical story into a long one, in the Ark of the Covenant lay a measurement rod. It was there as a reminder to all who ventured into Solomon's Temple that it is a valuable instrument, a divine measurement standard. The entire temple construction was based on this gauge, as instructed by God. I suspect Aaron's rod defined the lengths of both the cubit and the span: 524 mm for the cubit and exactly half of that, 262 mm, for the span. Poetic storytelling just got in the way of history, confusing the purely aesthetic with the practical reality of setting a building measurement standard.

Many years later, someone from a foreign land was looking at the Temple of Solomon with ill intentions. The idea was to destroy it, regardless of its beauty or spiritual significance, or perhaps because of its beauty and spiritual significance. Solomon's Temple sustained several attacks by foreign powers before finally, in 586 BCE, being totally destroyed by the army of Nebuchadnezzar II, the Babylonian king. The Ten Lost Tribes of Israel were then said to have been deported from the Kingdom of Israel after its conquest.

The tribes of Asher, Dan, Ephraim, Gad, Issachar, Manasseh, Naphtali, Reuben, Simeon and Zebulun were scattered to the four corners of the earth and became collectively known as the Ten Lost Tribes. To this day, various people from all over the world make claims of being descendants of these people. Legend has it that the return of the lost tribes, or their discovery, heralds the return of the Jewish Messiah. Jewish eschatology is concerned with events that will happen in the "end of days". This includes such things as the gathering in of the exiled diaspora and the coming of the Jewish Messiah and afterlife.

I suspect there may have been at least one person there at the time who had a sense of the impending calamity about to befall the Temple of Solomon. With the insight to prepare ahead of time, they devised a back-up strategy. In the dark of night our insightful member, one of the Ten Lost Tribes of Israel, headed north to where their Phoenician friends lived. They were carrying something of perceived great value to the people before it was destroyed or lost in the ensuing conflict. Their friend in Phoenicia had a boat. This ocean-going ship was about to go on a long journey west across the Mediterranean and beyond. It was the Phoenicians who had the skills and therefore the capacity to build the Temple of Solomon in the first place. The Bible describes Hiram of Tyre, the then leader of Phoenicia, who had supplied architects, tradespeople and cedar timbers for the building of the temple for his ally, Solomon, at Jerusalem. The Phoenicians were not particularly overjoyed about the temple being attacked, their artwork razed to the ground. They were planning another Ophir expedition anyway. They were eager to help. Being one of the most advanced seafarers in the world at the time, they had the capacity and therefore an obligation. Our Israelite convinced the captain they would be able to get the prized possessions through quarantine on the other side of the Atlantic. A visa shouldn't be a problem. A few months later, the Phoenician sailing ship ended up in the New World, America. It was carrying a perceived valuable cargo. Sailing by the currents and the wind, it ended up reaching the eastern seaboard of Central America somewhere in the Caribbean or the coast of what is now called Guatemala, Belize and Mexico.

Almost 2600 years later, an English naval captain entertained the notion that the Phoenicians were one of the first European civilisations to reach America by sea. Having built a replica to the identical design standard as that used in the biblical era around 600 BCE, this British naval officer hoped to cross the Atlantic Ocean. This journey, if successful, would suggest that Christopher Columbus, the Italian navigator and explorer, was way down the list as far as foreign arrival in the Americas. The captain has called his expedition Phoenicians Before Columbus.

I met Captain Philip Beale in Gosport in England and discussed my theory in brief. A few months later, in September 2019, by the winds of chance, there I was in Carthage, Tunisia. It was from this country that the *Phoenicia* was to begin its official voyage across the Atlantic Ocean

Image 16: Ancient ruins with the city of Tunis in the background, Tunisia, North Africa

Where am I? What am I doing here? What the hell am I doing here! Have I stuffed this up completely? These were the thoughts going through my mind. I was in this North African country with no idea where the *Phoenicia* was. Its onboard internet satellite tracking system had broken down. I knew it was somewhere between Spain and Tunisia and that it was heading my way into the wind, but that was it. No idea what port, what day, zero communication. Just guesswork. I had allowed about a six-day window for photographing this once-in-a-lifetime opportunity, after flying all the way from Australia. All I could do was wander around town and hope I tripped over somebody who knew what I was looking for. Every day was getting closer to when I had to depart, and I could not afford to stay there forever. Nobody at the marinas knew what planet I

Chapter 4 : I Was Here

was from when I said I was looking for a 2600-year-old sailing ship. I learned my first two words in Arabic, *shukraan*, meaning thank you, and *jamila*, meaning beautiful. I kept my Australian swearwords to myself.

Map 3: Tunis, Tunisia

Carthage in Tunis, Tunisia, was a major port for the ancient Phoenicians (Map 3). Founded in about the 9th century BCE on the coast of northwest Africa, it now lies between Algeria and Libya. One of a number of Phoenician settlements in the western Mediterranean, it was developed to facilitate trade from the city of Tyre, which is now in Lebanon. Carthage evolved into a significant trading empire throughout the Mediterranean, becoming one of the leading commercial centres of the western Mediterranean region by the end of the 7th century BCE.

The achievements of the Phoenicians have been somewhat neglected by historians. They were the first to discover purple dye. They invented glass blowing. They also invented the alphabet, which consisted of 22 letters; developed the art of open sea navigation; and developed a system of trading that did not involve war. Our civilisation has a lot to learn from them. After a long conflict known as the Punic Wars in 264–146 BCE, Rome finally destroyed Carthage in 146 BCE, establishing their own empire on the ancient ruins. Roman Carthage was then destroyed following its conquest by Arab invaders at the close of the 7th century CE. Carthage is now a suburb in the eastern part of Tunisia's capital city of Tunis.

By coincidence and with a little help from my daughter in England, I found a contact in government tourism who helped with my search.

*Image 17: The **Phoenicia** off the Mediterranean coast of Tunisia*

The arrival of the *Phoenicia* in Tunis turned into a significant event for the local tourism bureau, who saw it as an opportunity to hop on board for some publicity (Image 17). Suddenly I was swept up in a media event. I found myself being driven around the city in minibuses to historical sites and shouted to expensive restaurants with other journalists and filmmakers. I thought to myself, they must think I am more important than I really am. I went for the ride anyway.

Late one evening, when an English journalist friend and I were driven to our hotel by a high-level local government tourism representative and our female guide, I made one of my best, worst inappropriate comments. Driving along and looking for opportunities to make conversation, I saw a cat and asked how to say "cat" in Arabic, eager to add a third word to my extensive vocabulary. "Great! Now I know three words in Arabic," I said out loud. "*Shukraan, jamila* and *kus*." The response was not what I expected. It was suggested politely not to say those three words in that order, as it has a whole different connotation. "Thank you, beautiful pussy." I am very good at inappropriate comments; however, not so good at being an Australian diplomat in that particular instance. The next word I learned was *Asif,* "sorry".

Some people are going to be disgusted I ever repeated that story. Others will see the funny side. Humour is subjective. Inappropriatisms, which I call them, sometimes seem to roll off my tongue from out of the blue like chewing gum made of barbed wire.

Image 18: Phoenician ships were often adorned with a sculpture of a horse head in honour of their god of the sea, Yamm

The *Phoenicia* sailing ship had an atmosphere about it. It seemed as though it had a purpose, with a character of its own. It stood out where it was moored in the marina among all the expensive shiny yachts, attracting a crowd of onlookers. When I was on board in the marina, it was easy for me to imagine I had time travelled. I was back about 2500 years. Through the veil of centuries, I glimpsed people moving around the ship whom I thought could have been one of the Ten Lost Tribes. A clap of thunder peeled its way across the bow. With measurement rod in hand, otherwise known as Aaron's rod, they were setting off across the Atlantic Ocean to Central America. There they will meet the Maya. With a determination to share Solomon's wisdom, and with some artistic collaboration to integrate their philosophy with the Maya calendar, they will discuss their architectural measurement standard with their new-found friends.

But I noticed they were carrying something else with them. It looked like a 3-dimensional geometric shape of some kind. One of them held it up for me to see, but in a flash, it was gone. I could only just make it out as a storm blew in over Carthage from across the Mediterranean, thereby obscuring my vision. I had to wait about 2500 years to remember what it was.

I enjoy a little creative writing. As a journalist friend once said to me, some of the most fantastic, creative stories invariably have, as a foundation, some elements of truth and fact. This is an attempt to engage the reader. Not being a historian, I might not be able to provide all the dates and names from the era with accuracy. I could be as wrong or as right as the best of them by accident. My underlying aim with this book is to suggest a measurement gauge made its way across the Atlantic Ocean. By what means and with whom, I am not really sure. It is an enigma just like the Temple of Kukulkan itself. It is just such a strange coincidence the designers used an identical measurement. This is one possible reason why, I believe, Chichen Itza is designed like it is. This is the reason why the height of the steps is identical to half a cubit, exactly the length of a span of 262 mm. It was brought across the Atlantic Ocean. This length became the methodology used in scale measurement to incorporate time durations from the Maya calendar.

When I started this project, the question of what led to this measurement arriving in Central America was secondary for me. However, the more I looked into it, how it got there and who brought it there became increasingly intriguing for me. It was more than coincidental. I found the following reference from the biblical era, which provoked my curiosity even further. Esdras is the name of an apocalyptic book in many English versions of the Bible. Its authorship is ascribed to Ezra, a scribe and priest of the 5th century BCE:

> Those are the ten tribes, which were carried away prisoners out of their own land in the time of Osea the king, whom Salmanasar the king of Assyria led away captive, and **he carried them over the waters, and so came they into another land.**
>
> But they took this counsel among themselves, that they would

leave the multitude of the heathen, and go forth into a further country, **where never mankind dwelt**, ... (*King James Bible*, 1769/2020, 2 Esdras 13:40 & 13:41; emphasis added)

Where never mankind dwelt. Is that the Maya who lived across the Atlantic, which no one at the time knew about? I wonder.

Some interesting characters were on board the *Phoenicia* when I was there in Tunisia. There was a writer, one of three Mormons who planned to travel on the *Phoenicia*. He was in the process of writing a book. As I mentioned in Chapter 2, the Book of Mormon claims that the lost tribes travelled to the Americas and re-established a civilisation.

I became involved by coincidence in precisely what he was doing. He was setting out to document a part of history to support his belief system; I was investigating how a measurement system from biblical times travelled across the Atlantic Ocean. I was totally impartial with no reason or desire to prove any kind of religious agenda. I was operating on intuition or curiosity; perhaps automatic pilot may be a better term. It seemed remarkable to me that we were in Tunisia at the same time, and his view of ancient history began to stimulate my curiosity. I would have loved to go across the Atlantic on the *Phoenicia*; however, a planned trip to Guatemala already organised and paid for would not allow my finances to stretch that far.

Everything is back-to-front and upside-down. Twelve months before I set foot on board the *Phoenicia*, there I was, standing at the base of the Temple of Kukulkan, wondering why I was thinking about a Jewish connection. Even before I left Australia on holiday, I had this intuitive hunch. This was well before I had read much at all about Mesoamerican history; I was never particularly interested in the subject. This was also well before I ever heard of the *Phoenicia* sailing ship. I used to think the Maya calendar looked too complicated to bother studying. Jewish history was never a point of interest for me either, for that matter. It is now.

My feeling was, it is there concealed somewhere or somehow, but what is it? My intuition was on fire, without the kindling to fan the flame, without concrete evidence to back up an abstract thought pattern. How odd. Where is this coming from? What am I really doing in this place anyway? I'm remembering, that's what.

I suspect at some point in the last 3000 years, somebody from the Mediterranean region carried a measuring stick from across the Atlantic Ocean to Central America. It may have been the ancient Hebrews, or possibly the Phoenicians. On the other hand, it could have been the Egyptians. They were thought to incorporate time into architecture using the "pyramid inch". It may have been someone completely different. By some remarkable process, the royal cubit and the span became a standard measure used as a basis for design in architecture in Central America, specifically on the Temple of Kukulkan in Chichen Itza. It is my opinion that it was 524 mm long, made up of two divisions of 262 mm. Perhaps these were also broken down into smaller increments.

Today, these measurements are like a time capsule, a historical record of foreign arrival well before Christopher Columbus. Far more credible than an artefact that requires deciphering or carbon dating. This event from ancient history was preserved mathematically in architecture. Was it done on purpose by embedding the scale measurement in stone for safe-keeping? Was the intent to preserve the record of their arrival from being lost or destroyed, which could have happened if it were to exist in written form or relayed orally through generations?

To the people who brought this measurement rod across the Atlantic Ocean, it must have been of profound significance that their arrival, along with their unit of measurement, should be recorded and documented. They went to extraordinary lengths, excuse the pun, to encode the measurement in ratio and proportion. Just maybe this was in the hope that somebody from the future might eventually decipher the mathematics and therefore piece together a part of lost history.

I have reached my own conclusions as to who it was; however, I am leaving that observation for the final chapter of this book.

Mathematics enables one's capacity to perceive an event from ancient history that happened somewhere between one and three thousand years ago.

Chapter 4 : I Was Here

The Historical Value of Measurement

Image 19: Step height on the Temple of Kukulkan in spans and cubits m

The ancient Egyptian royal cubit (*meh niswt*) is the earliest attested standard measure, 524 mm in length (2 × 262 mm). A number of these rods have survived, found in the tomb of Maya from the 18th-century dynasty of the Pharaoh Tutankhamun in Saqqara, Egypt. The royal cubit was used from as early as the construction of the Step Pyramid of Djoser around 2700 BCE. The Egyptian span (*pedj-aa*) was half the length of the cubit, 262 mm.

The following is a re-examination of the proportions of the Temple of Kukulkan based on the royal cubit and span. Each step on the temple can be identified as a length of a span, and two steps designated the royal cubit. These measurements, once used in the Mediterranean, are over 4500 years old.

One span (Egyptian *pedj-aa*) = 1 step
Therefore, one span = 1 day
One cubit (Egyptian *meh niswt*) = 2 steps
Therefore, one cubit = 2 days

Image 20: Egyptian royal cubit, Department of Egyptian Antiquities, Louvre Museum

Image 21: The riser and tread combined measure as one cubit

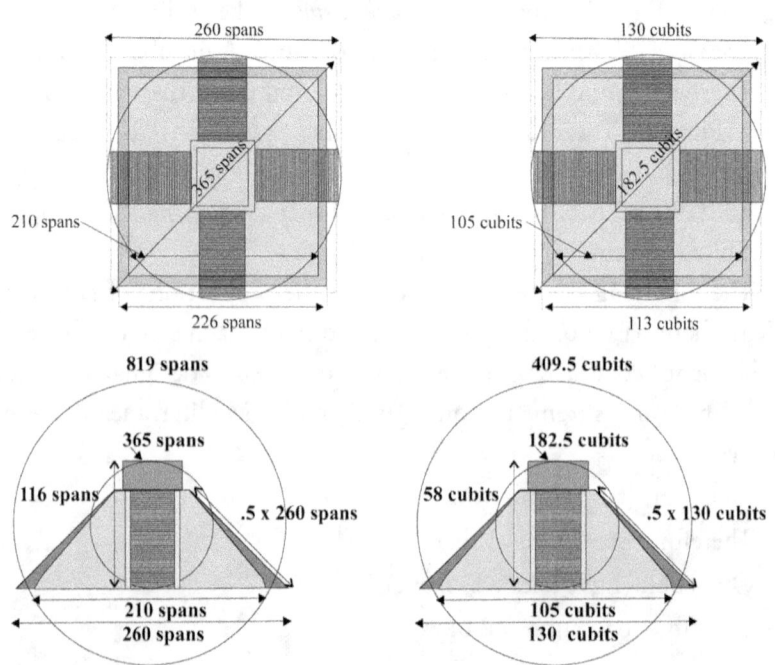

Diagram 23: Elevation and plan views showing dimensions in spans and cubits

Chapter 4 : I Was Here

For the ancient Israelites and the Egyptians, measurement was of critical significance to their worldview. Geometry and mathematics are conceptual constructions that these civilisations would have had in common. It is conceivable they would have exchanged knowledge about the importance of measurement standards because of their geographic proximity. The Great Pyramid on the Giza Plateau in Egypt has been analysed with considerable precision to reveal the recurring measurement now known as the royal cubit. The royal cubit and Ezekiel's cubit are identical in length. As far as my research is concerned, this measurement standard now extends to the design of the Temple of Kukulkan at Chichen Itza in Mexico.

In Mesopotamia, known as the birthplace of civilisation, measurement was also crucial to the functioning of their society and was held in high regard. Measurement was often depicted in sculpture as a rod and rope (Image 22). A rope is a useful tool with which to draw a circle. These two devices would have been instrumental in building the Temple of Solomon as well as the Maya temple.

Image 22: The stele of the Code of Hammurabi (Babylon) depicts the king holding what may be interpreted as a measurement rod

The following are some examples of biblical references to measurement.

> He took me there, and I saw a man whose appearance was like bronze; he was standing in the gateway with **a linen cord and a measuring rod** in his hand. (*Holy Bible, New International Version*, 1973/2020, Ezekiel 40:3; emphasis added)

> I was given **a reed like a measuring rod** and was told, "Go and **measure the temple** of God and the altar, with its worshipers". (*Holy Bible, New International Version*, 1973/2020, Revelation 11:1; emphasis added)

> The wall of the city had twelve foundation stones, and on them were the names of the twelve apostles of the Lamb. The angel who talked with me had a **measuring rod of gold to measure the city**, its gates and its walls. (*Holy Bible, New International Version*, 1973/2020, Revelation 21:14–15; emphasis added)

The Star of David and the Seal of Solomon

In the following pages, perhaps some of your belief systems are about to be challenged. Get ready.

The royal cubit is completely out of place in Mesoamerica. It is almost alien. It doesn't belong in Central America as far as the conventional history books would have us believe. Well, it doesn't stop with this measurement. There is something else alien to this landscape. I have discovered a geometric shape that is aligned perfectly with the architectural design of the Temple of Kukulkan, yet this is not supposed to be here either. No contemporary evidence of its use is recorded anywhere in Central America that I know of. Using mathematical evidence, I am suggesting the design of the Temple of Kukulkan is based on a symbol that has its own built-in controversy: a six-pointed star made up of two triangles. Along with the Maya calendar and the royal cubit, it is unmistakably at the very foundation of the entire construction layout. This can be proven mathematically.

The Star of David, which is composed of two interlocked equilateral triangles that form a six-pointed star, is almost instantly recognisable as a

Chapter 4 : I Was Here

symbol of Judaism. It appears on synagogues, Jewish tombstones and the flag of Israel. According to Encyclopedia Britannica, it was not until the 19th century that the star was universally adopted by Jewish communities as a striking emblem of Judaism (The Editors of Encyclopedia Britannica, 2020b). However, the origin of the symbol goes back in history well before that.

Another symbol from the biblical era is the Seal of Solomon. It is also known to have the same design of two triangles forming a six-pointed star; however, it varies slightly in appearance from the Star of David (Image 23).

Image 23: The Star of David and the Seal of Solomon

Star of David. *A symbol consisting of two* **overlapped** *equilateral triangles forming a star with six points, used as a symbol of Judaism. It is also called Magen David, Mogen David, and Shield of David, and is shaped identically to the hexagram and Solomon's seal. It is used on the flag of the modern state of Israel.* (Cassidy & Poznyakoff, n.d., Star of David, para. 3; emphasis added)

Solomon's seal. *A mystic symbol consisting of two* **interlaced** *triangles forming a star with six points, often with one triangle dark and one light, symbolic of the union of soul and body. It is shaped identically to the hexagram and Star of David, distinguished only in its usage.* (Cassidy & Poznyakoff, n.d., Solomon's seal, para. 1; emphasis added)

The Seal of Solomon is believed to be the signet ring worn by King Solomon, the son of David and Bathsheba. According to the Talmud,

King Solomon is one of the 48 prophets. In the Quran, he is considered a major prophet. Muslims refer to him by the Arabic variant, Sulayman, son of David. In the Hebrew Bible, King Solomon is credited as the builder of the First Temple in Jerusalem (also known as Solomon's Temple). Using the vast wealth he and his father had accumulated, he dedicated the temple to Yahweh, the God of Israel. He is portrayed as great in wisdom, wealth and power beyond either of the previous kings of the country. Solomon is the subject of many other later references and legends, most notably in the 1st-century work known as the Testament of Solomon. In the New Testament of the Bible, he is portrayed as a teacher of wisdom. In later years, Solomon also came to be known as a magician as well as an exorcist. Numerous medallion seals invoke his name. In a 2017 book, *Spirit Whirled: The Deaf Phoenicians*, Dylan Saccoccio claims that the name Solomon may be derived from *sol* (sun or son) and *mon* (moon). Other sources suggest it means "peace", from *shalom* in Hebrew and *Sulayman* in Arabic.

Back I go to the ever-faithful calculator, which has been a companion for years. It is my trusted archaeological tool to uncover the past. I actually do not get a lot of pleasure from mathematics, finding it confusing and annoying, disturbing even. Sometimes I absolutely hate it. However, I like the patterns forming once I get past the mesmerising effect of a million different alternatives and miscalculations. I love it especially here as I believe it has the potential to unravel one of the world's greatest mysteries from ancient history.

There are two parts to this odyssey I have found myself undertaking. Following on from the Maya calendar analysis, this chapter provides evidence suggesting that a scale measurement of 262 mm was used in accordance with a six-pointed-star pattern.

This became the basis of another journey into the mystery. The difficult question yet to be answered is, did people arrive in the New World with a six-pointed star, or was it already an integral part of Maya mathematics and geometric interpretation? Was evidence of the six-pointed star destroyed with the arrival of the Spanish? This, I cannot say. I cannot prove what the architects' understanding of the significance and relevance of the symbol was at the time. Was it mathematical or purely aesthetic?

Chapter 4 : I Was Here

Was it actually based on the Seal of Solomon? Did one of the lost tribes leave their indelible mark for future generations to discover? Considering the temple is based on a measurement equal to half a cubit, this additional information leaves the imagination to ponder the possibilities.

In the following diagrams, I put forward what I believe to be one of the most important discoveries of pre-Columbian archaeology and possibly the most controversial. As I write this, I feel that I cannot say it loud enough:

This is mathematical evidence that a six-pointed star serves as the basis of the design for the Temple of Kukulkan.

So here we go, proving the existence of a six-pointed star as a design feature.

I applied the Maya cycle of 819 days to a circle once again. Inside this circle is enclosed the Seal of Solomon. Lo and behold, the temple dimensions began to reveal themselves. Like a holy numerical shroud falling away from the rocks and mortar, the invisible mathematics shone through in all its geometric perfection. It was like walking through a jungle of arithmetic patterns and geometry to suddenly reveal the Chichen Itza temple hidden deep within all the calculations and mathematical analysis.

Diagram 24 on the following page shows the calculations derived from an inscribed six-pointed star enclosed within a circle with a circumference of 819 days. These results are then correlated with measurements of the Temple of Kukulkan. These numbers also have the same reference to the calendrical periods used by the Maya as those in Chapter 3. All measurements are in days to avoid confusion as we have already done the conversion from metres (see Table 1).

The first of several coincidences appeared: 225.3 days. This was almost exactly the side-length measurement of the small stone border around the perimeter of the building (226 days; see measurement K in Table 1). The surface has been replaced with what appears to be a layer of cement during the rectification of the temple. Maintaining the original structural integrity is one of the golden rules for a professional archaeologist.

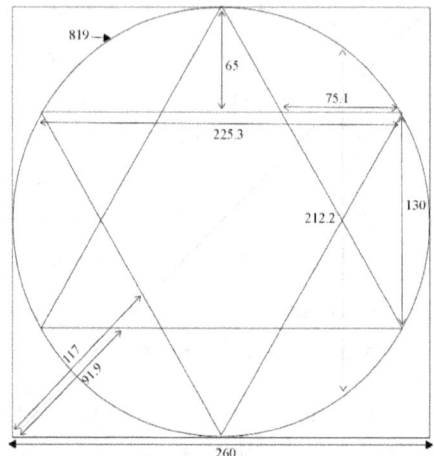

Diagram 24: Calculations derived from an inscribed six-pointed star enclosed within a circle with a circumference of 819 days

Image 24: The stone border around the perimeter of the temple

What I originally thought was a reference to the planet Venus, instead, or perhaps also, has its origins in the mathematical design of the Seal of Solomon. In Diagram 25, it can be seen how the geometry falls so perfectly into place. The significance of the placement of the stone border

Chapter 4 : I Was Here

around Chichen Itza becomes suddenly far less ambiguous, a variation of only 0.7 days, or 183 mm, from actual geometric measurements. This is over a length of more than 59 metres, so the accuracy is remarkable.

$$a = 2r \sin \frac{r}{n}$$

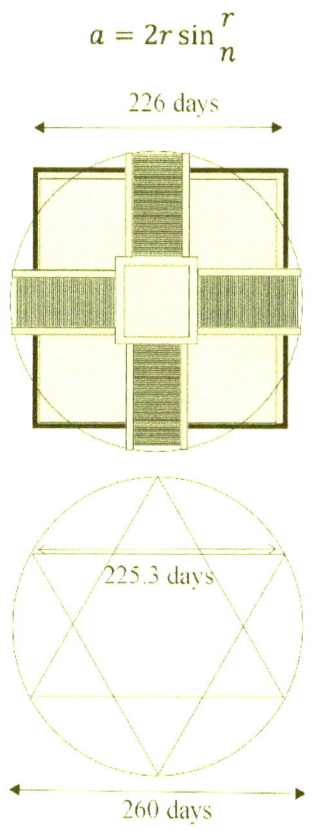

Diagram 25: *The length of the side of each triangle corresponds to the length of the stone border surrounding the temple*

This started the ball rolling. If this were the only corresponding measurement to be found, then the six-pointed star would not get a mention in this book. But there are more. It was not long before a length close to the 210-day cycle appeared, almost identical to one of the sides of the base of the pyramid (see Table 3 and Diagram 26). This is within 78 mm of true accuracy (with 210 days) over the entire width of the base of 55.1 m.

As shown in Table 3, the side lengths of the pyramid base vary between 55.1 m and 55.7 m, a range of 600 mm.

Table 3: Temple of Kukulkan pyramid base side lengths converted from metres to days

Base of pyramid	Side length (metres)	Conversion (millimetres)	No. of days
West face			
Left side	55.6	55,600/262	212.2 ≈ 210
Right side	55.7	55,700/262	212.6 ≈ 210
North face			
Left side	55.1	55,100/262	210.3 ≈ 210
Right side	55.2	55,200/262	210.7 ≈ 210

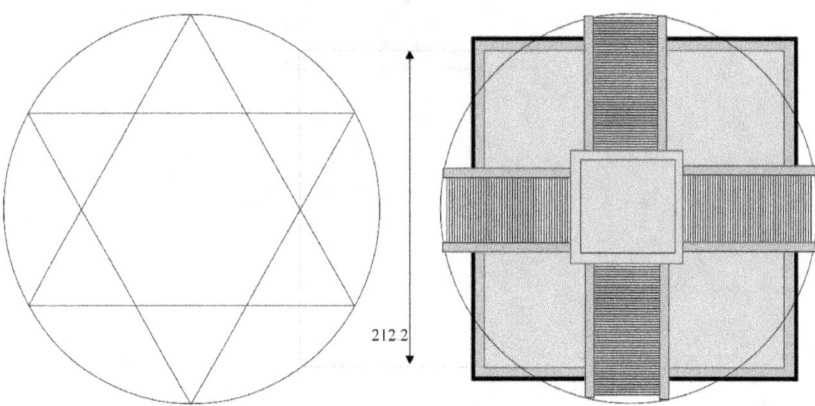

Diagram 26: The side lengths of the temple base correspond with the length of a line where it intersects with the circle

$$b = \sqrt{c^2 - a^2}$$
$$= \sqrt{260^2 - 150.2^2}$$
$$= 212.2$$

Or

$$b = \sqrt{c^2 - a^2}$$
$$= \sqrt{258^2 - 149^2}$$
$$= 210.6$$

Could it be that the designers intended the measurements of the base to represent multiple lengths, illustrating 212 days to address the geometry as well as 210 days for the calendar?

It became clearer to me that I was not manufacturing a mathematical reality. The builders of this Chichen Itza landmark have left behind a perfect six-pointed star in the design as evidence. If it was a link to an ancient Jewish heritage, could it be they set about concealing the evidence within its architectural design? Perhaps they may have had a premonition the conquistadors were on their way to make trouble. Like Nebuchadnezzar decades earlier, the conquistadors might have similar hobbies: that of extinguishing any record of this potent geometric symbol from ever being discovered. They certainly made sure almost all the Maya codices have vanished and with them any documented record of the use of a six-pointed star. This is where conspiracy theories start to develop if we allow them.

Quick! Hide it in the temple where it is invisible and yet in plain sight ... made visible by someone from the future. First, they will need to locate the measurement standard we used; next, determine how the calendar is encoded in the temple; and after doing that, understand the principles of the geometric symbol we used as the foundation. Then, they will remember who we were.

Was this part of the divine plan written in the scriptures? Is the Messiah coming forth to reclaim the lost tribes of Israel, thus returning them to the fold as foretold by ancient Hebrew mystics? Is this part of the restoration of Israel? All this, as the planet teeters on the edge of catastrophic climate change, according to scientific evidence.

Alternatively, and more simply, did the Maya just happen to use the six-pointed star as a mathematical design because they liked the shape?

These are some of the conflicts going through my mind as I write this book. This is why I thought it necessary to apologise pre-emptively. Some people may be upset about me implying the Maya were incapable of developing their own significant scientific concepts without foreign influence. I am not saying that. I am suggesting there may have been a collaboration of creative and intelligent minds. For others, any mention of Judaism or reinterpretation of their history brings up a heated response involving conspiracy theories, mistrust and all sorts of bizarre behaviour. Regardless, back to the calculator I went.

I decided to dissect the Seal of Solomon, or the Star of David, or whatever you would like to call it, a bit further. Other significant measurements confirmed my original intuitive hunch.

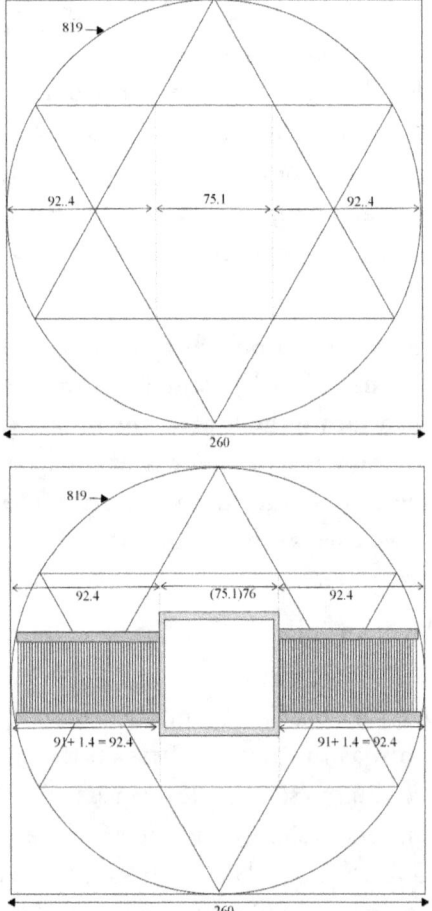

Diagram 27: The width of the elevated platform is almost the same as the intersecting points within a six-pointed star

I see Diagram 27 as significant evidence. The side of the platform (76 days) is almost the same as the length to the intersection point. These measures are almost identical. The six-pointed star produces a length of 92.4 days to the intersection. The steps are set back from the end of the stringers (see detail of steps in Diagram 20, Chapter 3). This allows for the variation between 92.4 and the 91 steps in the actual architecture.

Equivalent measures from the Chichen Itza temple are recurring with consistency, too many to be a coincidence. The width of the stairway that rises to the elevated platform (measurement N in Table 1) is 8.5 m or 32.6 (± 0.1) days. This is exactly half the size of the small triangles, as shown in Diagram 28.

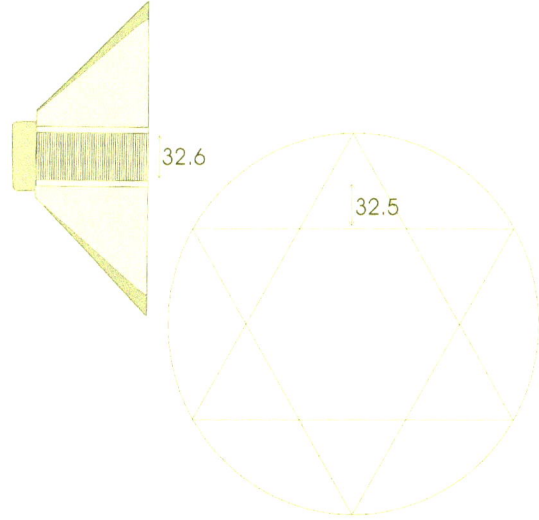

Diagram 28: The width of the steps is exactly half the height of the small triangles

The width of the steps including the stringer width (measurement O in Table 1) is 11.9 m or 45.4 days, almost exactly half the height to the elevated platform (measurement G in Table 1). As shown in Diagram 29, both the overall height and the height to the elevated platform correspond to measurements within a six-pointed star.

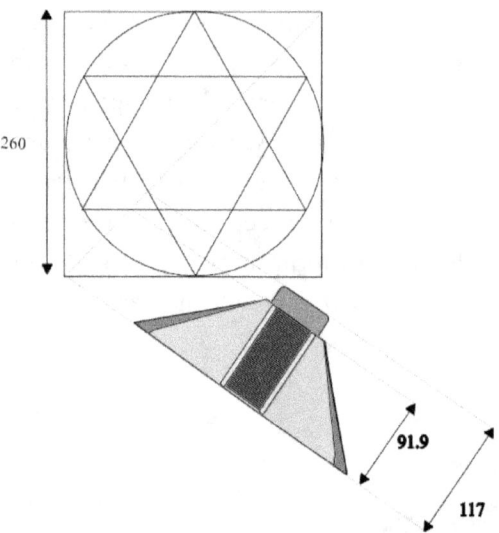

Diagram 29: The overall height and the height to the elevated platform correspond to measurements within a six-pointed star

According to my estimation, the Star of David reveals measurements from both a plan and an elevation perspective (Diagram 30).

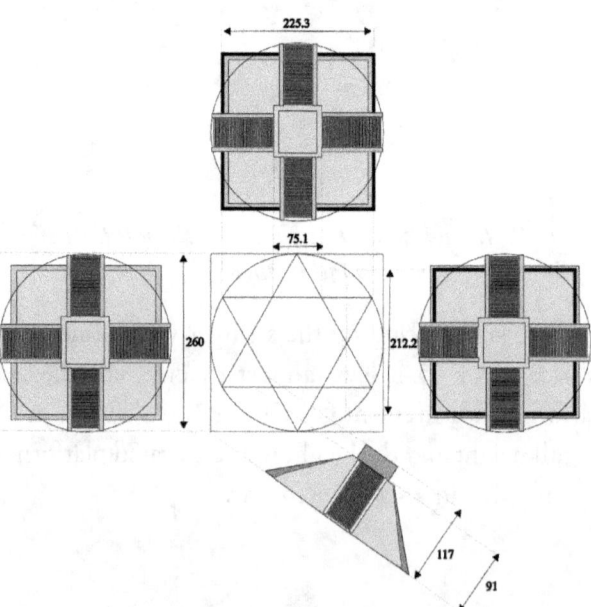

Diagram 30: This composite diagram shows how the six-pointed star relates to the dimensions of the Temple of Kukulkan

Chapter 4 : I Was Here

$$91.9 = \sqrt{65^2 + 65^2}$$

and

$$260 \times \sqrt{2} \div 4 = 91.9 \approx 91$$

- Actual number of steps on Chichen Itza: 91
- Geometric equivalent: 91.9
- Height of Kukulkan: 116 days
- Geometric equivalent: 117

I don't have the trigonometry skills to calculate the 117-day measurement in the six-pointed star. I cheated and used a CAD (computer-aided design) drawing program where I was able to calculate the measurement with some degree of accuracy. I will have to leave that for someone with more mathematical skills than I currently have to calculate.

Identical measurements to the cycles in the Maya calendar can be found in the Temple of Kukulkan. Measurements contained in a six-pointed star can be found in the corresponding proportional dimensions of the Temple of Kukulkan with over 99% accuracy.

Image 25: The main temple on the elevated platform

Table 4: Comparison of Temple of Kukulkan measurements with six-pointed star measurements

Kukulkan reference from Table 1	Kukulkan measurement (metres = days)	Six-pointed star measurement (days)	Variation	% error	Variation millimetres (one day = 262 mm)
K: Stone border (side length)	59.2 = 226.0	225.3	0.7	0.31	262 × 0.7 = 183 mm
E: Base of pyramid (mean side length)	55.4 = 211.5	212.2	0.7	0.33	262 × 0.7 = 183 mm
N: Stairway width	8.53 = 32.6	32.5	0.1	0.31	262 × 0.1 = 26.2 mm
L: Elevated platform (side)	19.9 = 76.0	75.1	0.9	1.18	262 × 0.9 = 235.8 mm
G: Height to platform	23.9 = 91.2	91.9	0.7	0.77	262 × 0.7 = 183 mm
F: Overall height	30.4 = 116.0	117.0	1.0	0.86	262 × 1.0 = 262 mm

Who Was Here?

Who is the face looking out across the open spectacle of Chichen Itza with an ever-watchful eye (Image 25)? Is it the designer immortalised in stone? Perhaps it is meant to represent Kukulkan himself. Why is the rectangle enclosing the face 7 spans wide and therefore 3.5 cubits? Why is it exactly 7 steps (or days) in width?

$$1.834 \text{ m} \div 0.262 = 7 \text{ days}$$

The number seven was considered divinely perfect by the ancient Hebrews with, for instance, the seven days of the creation. This number was also used to swear an oath or a *Shvua*, sometimes known as *Sheva*. It is considered a holy number mentioned numerous times in the Bible. There are seven candles on the Menora.

For the Maya, nearly all the monuments on the Yucatán Peninsula show evidence that they also had a fascination with this number. Their artificial mounds were composed of seven superimposed platforms; kings and queens were adorned with seven blue feathers on their headdress. The number seven prevails in many places where Maya influence has predominated.

I have left out analysing the measurements of the elevated temple in detail simply because I do not have access to the 3-dimensional lidar scans anymore. Therefore, I am not able to measure the inside dimensions. I am guessing it would be related to a smaller six-pointed star enclosed within the larger one. If I ever get the technical assistance to do an investigation, I will. The results can then be posted on the net as a supplement to this existing research. For now, it is available for anyone who may feel inclined to do their own investigation. Or perhaps the time is not yet right to enter the temple. Could it be there are not yet enough people on planet Earth who have experienced a personal transformation to allow for a total shift in consciousness? Perhaps a tipping point is required and, as a result, growth in intuitive knowledge and wisdom becomes exponential, involving the entire world population.

The Temple of Solomon

My curiosity was stimulated to the point of no return. The temple had, for me, acquired a whole new perspective. Its enigmatic qualities kept getting more intriguing. The six-pointed star, a symbol definitely identifiable with the Mediterranean region, had found its way to Mesoamerica along with the royal cubit. This led me to investigate documented dimensions of the Temple of Solomon to see how they compared with those of the Temple of Kukulkan.

Solomon's Temple was destroyed twice: once in 586 BCE, rebuilt to become what is known as the Second Temple, and then demolished again by the Romans. Jewish temple building is not what you would call a permanent success story. There is now a movement in Israel to build a third temple, with considerable discussion about exactly where and when.

Sacred sites from ancient history usually had one thing in common. Invariably, they had the cosmos in mind with regard to design or orientation. In places such as Egypt and Stonehenge, in England, it would be virtually inconceivable to construct any place of worship without consideration of the alignment with astronomy. They just did that back then. Yet, according to my research, there remains an inconsistency with Solomon's Temple. There is a complete lack of historical references indicating it had any links to astronomy in its orientation or design. The only reference I can find is that the entrance might have faced east, which would have it facing toward the equinox. Surrounding megalith sites such as Ain Dara in Syria, the Great Pyramid in Egypt, and so on, all have design features relating to astronomy. Just its name, Solomon, implies the design may have had interaction with the sun and the moon, since the name could be derived from *sol* (sun) and *mon* (moon). Was the temple named after the king or the other way around?

This was the primary temple of the Jewish people. The Phoenicians built Solomon's Temple using many of their design practices. There would have been influences from the Egyptians, who were known for their knowledge of astronomy and its application in building the pyramids. The design plan of Solomon's Temple needs a little more interrogation from this perspective, perhaps throwing light on the intent of its dimensions. A quick look at the mathematics may provide an answer.

I found a curious common denominator in the size comparison between the two structures. Conversion of the height of Kukulkan to cubits equals 58 cubits (116 spans/days divided by 2). This is only 2 cubits or 1048 mm short of the length of Solomon's Temple, which by most accounts is 60 cubits long. Should the width of the walls be considered a factor, and if they were each about 262 mm thick, then the interior length would be almost identical to the height of the Temple of Kukulkan. This is using the royal cubit of 524 mm in length. Then again, if the walls were 1 cubit thick, the comparative measure would be identical.

The standard width of a concrete block used in construction in Australia is 190 mm. A wall width of 262 mm is not out of the question. Considering the Temple of Solomon was built 2500 years ago, it

Chapter 4 : I Was Here

is reasonable to suggest a wall 1 cubit in width would not be out of the question, either.

Diagram 31 below shows the relative proportions.

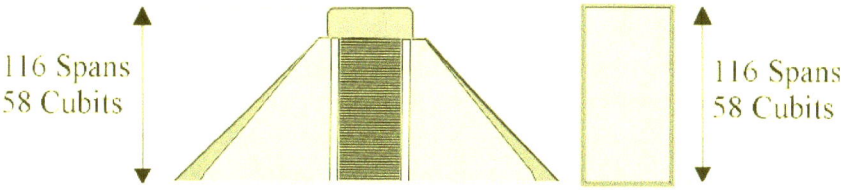

Diagram 31: Solomon's Temple possible internal length as compared to the height of the Temple of Kukulkan

The Temple of Solomon has a mathematical similarity to the Temple of Kukulkan—another enigma to add to the growing list. Perhaps a Hebrew rabbi already knows of the astronomy connections to Solomon's Temple. Or perhaps Israel's history is similar to that of the Maya civilisation, with all records contained in the Temple of Solomon systematically destroyed along with the temple itself.

Other similarities include that the Temple of Solomon is believed to be built over the Gihon Spring. The Temple of Kukulkan is constructed over a waterhole called a cenote. This is a subject deserving of a more in-depth study all on its own, but not here.

The salient question from this investigation is: Did the builders intentionally leave clues so that they could be reinterpreted at some distant time in the future? The mind boggles. To recap:

- The unit of measurement in the Temple of Kukulkan is identical to that used in the Temple of Solomon.
- That unit of measurement relates to time periods from the Maya calendar.
- The six-pointed star forms the geometric basis of the design.
- The length of the Temple of Solomon is almost identical to the height of the Temple of Kukulkan.

Chapter 5

The Neurotransmitter Fix

As part of expanding this investigation to more remote areas of Central America other than Mexico, I set out to explore further afield, deep within the homeland of the ancient Maya. Guatemala and Honduras are the main regions where this civilisation first evolved. I was curious to see if I could find either the 262 mm measurement or the cubit length built into architecture elsewhere in Central America.

Image 26: Late afternoon, Tikal, Guatemala

Chapter 5 : The Neurotransmitter Fix

Being unable to locate a stylised Indiana Jones whip, I set off with a measuring tape from the local hardware store. All that had to be done was to compare the height of some steps with the measurements I found at Chichen Itza. Several thousand stone structures were built throughout the jungle over the last couple of millennia. If only I could be so lucky as to find one good example. Imagine that, finding a six-pointed star carved in stone in a lost cave. If tangible evidence were to appear, that would really set the cat among the pigeons, historically speaking. At the time of writing this, I have not found substantial proof documented anywhere that the Maya ever used the six-pointed star. It seems to be culturally incongruent. However, I have heard that the Star of David was found carved on rock in Uxmal and Campeche, Mexico, and also in Tikal, yet there is no strong visual evidence to back up these claims. The internet is full of misinformation, and I am not going to add to it by providing any fabricated stories in this book. Unless I see it with my own eyes or can photograph it with my camera, it is not relevant.

It is only speculative for me to say that the ancient Israelis or the Phoenicians took their measurement and geometry to the New World—just opinion based on mathematical analysis. I do have a fairly strong viewpoint on this discipline being the key to understanding the past. So, I will also have an eye out for the sacred Seal of Solomon. In my peripheral vision, I might glimpse something that will lead me on the right path. I am basically an optimist. Something good will come of this.

There was a little bit of anxiety associated with travelling to Guatemala. It is on the pathway for refugees travelling from El Salvador and Honduras on their way to seek a better life in the USA. There were reports of kidnappings and robbery. The Australian travel website warned about exercising a high degree of caution as some areas are under a state of emergency. However, my affirmation when travelling is this: leave my fear at home and pack my common sense. "Beware of excessively friendly types" is my personal motto when travelling. The ones who sidle up to you and appear so nice and helpful. More often than not, they are looking for an easy ride, and one thing I know about myself is that I am a soft target. Most people in Guatemala are survivalists. They have to be. There are limited social services in place with abundant poverty.

So, to the land of the eternal spring I went in search of evidence, with some degree of trepidation. I knew it would be a long shot; the chances were remote. The odds were against me. But my curiosity got the better of me; I went anyway. It was a hot night in September 2019 when I landed in Guatemala City. I didn't know a soul in the entire country.

> Furthermore, we have not even to risk the adventure alone; for the heroes of all time have gone before us; the labyrinth is thoroughly known; we have only to follow the thread of the hero-path. And where we had thought to find an abomination, we shall find a god; where we had thought to slay another, we shall slay ourselves; where we had thought to travel outward, we shall come to the center of our own existence; where we had thought to be alone, we shall be with all the world. (Joseph Campbell, 1949, p. 18)

I found my way to my hotel, which was inconveniently shut at 2 o'clock in the morning. The taxi driver persisted with a loud knock on the door as a group of youths jostled with one another a short distance away. *Open, please open.* I did not need any dramas on my first day there. Eventually, it did. To my relief, a four-bed room relieved my jetlagged state of mind.

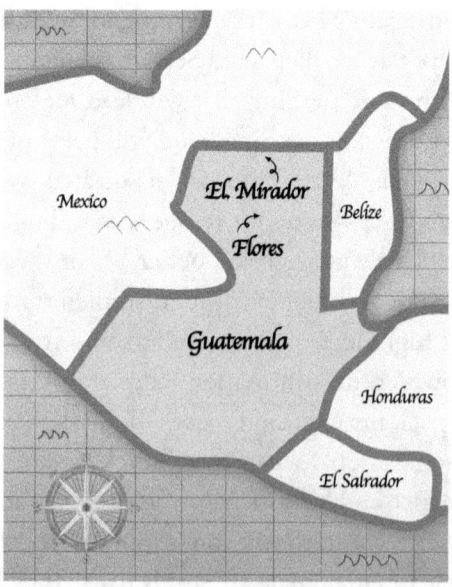

Map 4: Map of Guatemala showing location of Flores and El Mirador

Chapter 5 : The Neurotransmitter Fix

I had a window of about three or four weeks. Factoring in travel between destinations, that amount of time was broken down to about eight days. Those days were reduced still further when considering getting to the temples and then walking the pathways in between. Therefore, I estimated I had less than 20 or 30 hours of quality investigation time. I had plenty of optimism but very little time to find some support for my theory. All this on a limited budget. It would require a miracle. However, I expect miracles to appear. I just need to recognise what form they might take.

Image 27: Yaxhá Lake is situated in northern Petén, Guatemala

I had a comprehensive vocabulary of about two words in Spanish that I knew off by heart: *mañana*, meaning tomorrow, and *gracias*, thank you. Now I could speak two or three words in two different languages. These two words quickly evolved into a third one, *caliente*, meaning hot. That is an understatement. The heat is omnipresent in this country, except in the highlands to the south-west.

The internet translator became my friend. The odd thing for me was, here in Guatemala, I became an "it". By some strange, twisted digital reinterpretation, often when trying to communicate, something went wrong in the translation. "Does it want sugar with the coffee?" "Where is it going today?" I already had a bit of an identity crisis, but this was not helping.

"So, are you going to build your own pyramid?" an American tourist quipped as I frantically tried to measure the height of the steps on a temple at Yaxhá in the Petén region in northern Guatemala (Images 28 and 29). "I might," I whispered to myself. How confusing is this going to be: photograph the temple steps, measure as many as possible to get the average, remember what I just did, document it and try and keep up with the tour group at the same time. All this in the oppressive heat where all you want to do is lie down in the shade. Impossible dream. One step that measured exactly 262 mm caught my attention. But alas, that was the only one. A quick survey of the rest of the area proved nothing consistent. The steps had irregular heights and substantial erosion. Disappointingly, there was nothing "it" could find here in Yaxhá on "its" first very uncomprehensive survey.

Image 28: Classic Maya pyramid, Yaxhá

I don't usually like tour groups. There is always "the one". The person who is a generally disruptive troublemaker of some kind, who is determined to be difficult to get along with. Thankfully, on this entire trip the excursions usually lasted only a few hours, and then we all went in our separate directions. We were not together long enough to learn to dislike each other uncontrollably.

Chapter 5 : The Neurotransmitter Fix

Image 29: The author measuring steps in the ruins of Guatemala

On the way back from Yaxhá, hot, sweaty and desiring a shower, I chatted with the tour guide, Oswaldo. Also known as Antonio Dias, he was a 64-year-old Maya who was fluent in several languages and the father of 12 children. What did he just say?

"The Mayan word for calendar is a Jewish word."

"What!" I said. He went on, "But you will have to check it out."

How on earth am I going to do that? I know nothing about the Mayan language. Nor can I speak Hebrew. This particular aspect of my investigation seems too big for me to take on. Is it a rumour, a red herring? Later, I discovered there were about 23 separate dialects of the Mayan language spoken in Guatemala alone. The same number as there are volcanoes. Am I going to investigate this any further? No, far too complicated in this current attempt.

I still haven't found what I am looking for.

I returned to my hotel in the idyllic setting of the island of Flores (Image 30). So tranquil and peaceful, yet this place comes with a chequered past. It was the last Maya stronghold in the entire region. The Spanish invaded the island, destroying whatever evidence there was of the original inhabitants. The surviving Maya swam off toward the mainland, hiding in the jungle. What exists now is typical Spanish-style buildings, disappointingly, with no Maya influence whatsoever.

Image 30: Flores is a town situated on an island in Guatemala's northern Petén region

Regional Guatemala

It was on the Island of Flores, known to the original Maya as *Nojpetén*, where I met a young man who was of Maya and Spanish ancestry. I was invited to go with him and his partner from Texas, USA, to meet his uncle who lived in a regional rural community. I have heard rumours of kidnapping, murder and similar adventures about travelling off the beaten track in Guatemala. I did not know these people at all; however, I saw this as an opportunity, albeit high risk. Perhaps I might be led to a hidden cave where displayed on the wall was the Seal of Solomon. In a secret temple in the rainforest, there might be a measuring rod with strange hieroglyphics detailing the days of the year. I decided to go because I have chosen to live life on the edge, not too close, yet close enough to sample the unexpected. Risk assessment factor ... about 7 out of 10.

My archaeology excursion into unknown territory turned out to be something totally unexpected.

Chapter 5 : The Neurotransmitter Fix

Image 31: The Guatemalan public transport known locally as a chicken bus

With a few loose teeth after a bumpy six-hour ride on what is called a chicken bus (Image 31), and then on a tuk-tuk down a dusty road, we arrived at his uncle's house. There, I was to spend the next two nights. I met the uncle and his wife, whom I will call Alejandro and Nardia to maintain their privacy. I soon learned that this was a household with tragedy embedded in its walls. This couple had lost one of their sons, who was shot dead at the age of 20. Alejandro had a subsequent breakdown and turned to alcohol to deal with his grief. He has now resumed his life, recovering somewhat from the ordeal. Is that possible? Can a parent ever recover from the loss of a child?

What started out as a journey into the jungles of Guatemala in search of my goal required a rapid reorientation. My heart went out to these gentle, quietly spoken people living near a remote village in a house with no running water and a dirt floor. Nearby, a river supported the family and the local community, as it had for thousands of years. Alejandro was a fisherman.

These people were contemporary Guatemalans. They were living mostly off the land, yet not living by the Maya calendar as their ancestors would have done. Many Maya people still live traditionally using ancient ceremonial practices in the south-western highlands, some of whom only speak their own dialect. Electricity was about to arrive at their house for the first time. They had a dirt floor and mosquitoes were plentiful.

Image 32: A typical house with thatched roof in regional Guatemala

Their daughter, Oriana (also a pseudonym), lived in a house next door on a small block of land about two acres in size. She had two children from a current marriage and two from a previous one. She hadn't seen her older children for seven years. They were taken to America by her ex-partner.

Image 33: Laundry day at a nearby creek

Chapter 5 : The Neurotransmitter Fix

The walls of the house were stained with tears. That is typical of Guatemala, a fertile land where suffering and loss is not uncommon.

> **Occasionally the universe throws mud in our eyes in the form of tragedy. Immediately in pain and blinded, the pathway forward is obscured and seemingly impossible to negotiate. Little by little, the pain eases. Gradually over time, tears clear our vision and somehow, somewhere, if we are lucky, we may have an opportunity to glimpse the perfection of the universe.**

The experience made me feel a little self-obsessed. Here I am preoccupied with finding evidence to support my theory and then I meet a family who, deep within their soul, continuously search for reasons why their children have been taken away. Their preoccupation, their search, is omnipresent. Mine is superficial and almost inconsequential by comparison.

I was getting my first taste of regional Guatemala, a land where numerous people don't know who their father is. I saw lots of girls who looked about 16 years old with infants. By Western standards, one could easily say there was a fair amount of social dysfunction in regional areas. There was no evidence of starvation; in fact, obesity is widespread, excuse the pun. I also saw beautiful open smiles and gentle, kind and generous people. I saw a land of difficulty, hardship, poverty, and yet, in shared adversity, the community gathers around each other in support.

On a different excursion, I met a traveller from Israel. This young fellow told me that here, in this country, Jewish people feel welcome to travel. Usually, he said, when abroad in other countries, he finds people somewhat standoffish as soon as he mentions his nationality. In Guatemala, he feels there is not that prejudice. It was one of the first countries to recognise Jerusalem as the capital of Israel. I find this curiously interesting in light of my search for the possible ancient Hebrew connections to this land.

The Steel Is Tempered in the Mud

Mosquitoes and tropical slush in 90% humidity. That was the environment on a 17-kilometre slow trot carrying two cameras, water and a tripod through the mud on the first day of a trek totalling 91 kilometres.

I was in the remote jungle in northern Guatemala bordering Mexico, wondering if I was going to survive this adventure. What on earth have I got myself into again? The first day we travelled at a ridiculous speed. My six companions were on average about 27 years old. Why are we moving at a gallop through the jungle? Is there a McDonald's restaurant about to close somewhere that I didn't know about? They moved with grace and ease over fallen logs, ducking and weaving past overhanging brambles and making it all look like so much fun. They made me feel like a stumbling tapir trying to keep up.

I was ticking the final box. You know, the section where you mark your age: 20–30, 30–40, 40–50, then you get to the final one, 51+. How did this happen so fast? There are no more boxes to tick after this one.

Image 34: The mule and guide walking through the mud and slush

That was the first day of a total of five on the trek overland to a mystical place that beckoned me to explore. This is what I dreamed of. I am here in search of a place that not many people know about. Somewhere hidden, isolated, a secret place where all the mysteries of a lost, forgotten world are kept safe from the prying eyes of the hungry mobs. But why are we in such a bloody hurry to get there? I nicknamed our guide, Alfonzo, "the rabbit". This was a seriously fast walk in the humid tropical heat, through the mud and rain. Even the mules had a distressed, quizzical look on their faces. Was it delirium and fatigue that made me feel like I had recognised the face of one mosquito among the millions? It looked somehow familiar, leaving me wondering how it got all the way here from Australia. Later I learned we had to go quickly to beat nightfall as we'd had a late start at the small town of Carmelita where the trek originated from. The next day was worse, 24 kilometres on foot.

In the jungles of northern Guatemala lies the most mysterious sight. Almost mystical. No, definitely mystical. La Danta, the largest pyramid in the world by volume (Image 35). This is a handmade artwork. The Maya never used the wheel as far as we know. Blood, sweat and tears built this mountain elevated far above the surrounding treetops. It was physical hardship in this remote environment that must have fashioned the people of the Maya civilisation. From up here on high, the shamans and mystics raised their intuitive capacity to see far off into the future, beyond the veil … beyond the illusion … beyond the Maya.

Image 35: One of the largest pyramids in the world, La Danta pyramid in northern Guatemala

We all found it virtually impossible to comprehend the full scale of the civilisation that once thrived here. There are estimated to be about 26 known archaeological sites in the region, of which only 14 have been studied. Another 30 or so more await excavation. Some say thousands, possibly millions of people once lived in this now-abandoned mega-city, of which only a portion has been restored. These estimated statistics are based on studies of 3-dimensional images produced by lidar aerial surveying.

Image 36: The thick rainforest where an ancient civilisation once thrived at El Mirador, abandoned almost 2000 years ago

We explored the possibility it would take thousands of workers (or perhaps slaves) to build something like this. However, our social system is our primary reference point. Our society, our civilisation is based on people either being paid for services rendered or coerced to work under forced labour. Sadly, that's our worldview. It is all about the money. How much does it cost? Could it be that this ancient society functioned differently, as a totally collaborative effort? Imagine that, the entire workforce freely contributing, aligned together for the building of something monumental, for the spiritual wellbeing of every member of the community—no whingeing or complaining, no sick days without having an authentic excuse, nobody feeling like they are taken advantage of.

This was a primal archaeological zone devoid of tourists except for us and our guides. However, occasionally the throbbing sound of a helicopter would break the quiet as a group of tourists descended from the clouds for a short stay. By night, we had the jungle to ourselves where the call of the howler monkeys could be heard above the silence. This relatively small primate has mastered the art of sound projection. Their eerie, primal sound seems to travel way beyond their small physical bodies, as though it is captured by the humid atmosphere. It is projected through the treetops and then carried across this mysterious landscape. What an incredible sound to be woken up by in the middle of the night.

Image 37: Detailed artwork from a lost civilisation

Image 38: A howler monkey rests in the forest canopy

The once-popular ball game played in the area by the ancient Maya has now been replaced with another recreational sport, smoking pot. Marijuana is commonplace in Guatemala, especially deep within the northern jungle areas of Petén. I glanced at the donkeys heaving our luggage through the mud, which I occasionally noticed were laughing at nothing. I soon realised that must be where the term "drug mule" comes from.

The final age box on the form has very little in common with any of the previous ones. My humour usually went over my companions' heads. They were just nice young people, full of adventure, full of life. They were out having a good time, walking along, voices at high volume, not a care in the world. Every animal within ten miles would have beaten a hasty retreat. I didn't want to be "the one". I refused to be the trouble-maker disrupting it for the rest of the group by stating the obvious. Yet the generation gap was a definite challenge for me. The conversation is different—the values, worlds apart. But we were bonded permanently by the intensity of the physical challenge. Here we were, on the precipice of time looking back to when the world was different. Perhaps a lot saner than it is now.

Image 39: My travelling companions

It is believed deforestation brought an end to the Maya civilisation that built some of the largest pyramids on the planet. Trees attract rain. Without rain, there is no water in a region that already lacked a permanent water source. We considered the possibility that thousands of years ago, the climate change debate polarising the planet now was also active within this ancient Maya community. If we keep destroying the environment, the obvious will happen. Did their climate change sceptics eventually meet their fate as a result of their very own argument, along with the rest of the population? Too many people, not enough resource … cull the population perhaps. The mythical land of El Mirador surrendered to environmental destruction; it is believed the surviving inhabitants moved to the Western Highlands of Guatemala.

I contemplated the possibility that, in the quest toward spiritual heights and artistic sensibility, they may have gone a little too far, where there becomes a disconnection with reality and practicality. That is something I had to be careful about myself.

Standing on the mountain of time, we look back across the historical plain behind us, measure the pathway already travelled and sense the one that lies before us.

On an excursion to a nearby pyramid, I chose to wait at the bottom as the journey there was already enough for my exhausted legs. I sat at the base while the rest of my noisy companions ascended the pyramid. Only a few minutes had elapsed when I heard something in the bushes about 10 metres away. It was a feral pig and was as shocked to see me as I was it. It didn't waste any time disappearing.

I realised something about nature at that moment. When animals hear the sound of humans, they avoid contact and wait for the danger to pass. Then they come out a short time later, thinking it is safe to do so provided they can hear the sound receding. I used this experience the next day on another excursion.

Like the previous day, I waited on the pathway while my young friends went to the top of a temple to see the sunset. They went ahead on their merry way, singing and laughing. I sat motionless on a log. My trap was laid for any unsuspecting wildlife that may appear.

The crescendo of the mobile band of noisy humans moved off into the jungle. With them went the sound of about 10,000 mosquitoes. I anticipated something would happen, and it did. A type of deer appeared in the distance, unaware I was there. As darkness gradually enveloped us, the deer was swallowed up by the forest. Silently, I waited on the pathway hoping that an unsuspecting jaguar would come into view. I waited and waited. The howler monkeys went quiet. I couldn't see a thing. I had started out thinking I was going to be the one doing the watching; however, as night fell, it seemed I could be the one being watched. Setting my camera to automatic flash, I occasionally fired off a random shot in all four directions just in case a predator had me in their sights. If this is the place where I die, then I go doing what I do best, chasing illusions.

Then I noticed something in the camera review shots. Small points of light recorded in the digital image that I knew were not reflections. I was not alone. This was a familiar image; I had photographed these before. They are called orbs.

Image 40: A photograph of an orb, with enlargement

Orbs, sometimes known as ghost orbs, are a controversial paranormal phenomenon (Image 40). I have read they are evidence of active spiritual energy, where the spirit is telling the living that some kind of significant event happened at that location. Most certainly, there would have been spiritual activity at the site of La Danta, the largest pyramid in the world

Chapter 5 : The Neurotransmitter Fix

by volume. Orbs are said to be spirits from the astral plane that allow themselves to be photographed. Sceptics will say they are just a refraction of light on the camera lens. They were not visible to the naked eye. I am not here to convince anyone either way. In fact, I don't really care what people think. That is one benefit with ticking the final box. Polarised viewpoints, polarised opinions, that's all we seem to base our worldview on. However, I believe I was in the right place for an event like this to occur, at the base of a temple almost 3000 years old, miles from anywhere.

Perhaps orbs appear when an individual is in need of assistance from a divine source. They let the person know they are being helped. I needed all the help I could get. My feet were killing me. My sciatica was like a poison dart lodged in my hip. I had just slow-trotted over 45 kilometres through the jungle, including various excursions to nearby temples, to be at this place. The return journey was still in front of me. I achieved my personal best at trekking, which is not my forte. Perhaps, I was not alone doing this. There was some eerie comfort in that.

There is a Maya legend of little spirit people called the Alux (pronounced "aloosh"), which are said to be less than three feet tall. It is believed shamans can cast ritual spells to bring highly detailed clay figures to life and they become the Alux. From talking to Maya people, I have learned it is best to be on good terms with these beings as they can make trouble and mischief for a household. They have been assigned some degree of power and are considered to be very real even to many contemporary Maya. I wondered if orbs are the beginnings of these mythical little beings. I quickly put that thought out of my mind.

Surely with all this spiritual activity, something will come to light for all my effort?

In the homeland of the Snake Kings, La Danta reaches up through the rainforest as though aching for the sunlight. Its height is estimated to be 71.9 m. I began a mental comparison of measurements. This height is 4.3 m more than the width of the Temple of Kukulkan at Chichen Itza (67.6 m). Could the modern surveyors of La Danta have measured it from the wrong level? That would be an easy mistake as the topography of the ground surface is irregular and covered with centuries of foliage. Is 68.1 m, and therefore 260 days, the actual intended height, using the scale measurement of 262 mm? Did someone make a mistake? Am I making a mistake? Was there no connection at all? El Mirador was at its peak around the 6th century BCE and then later in what is called the late Classic period. Chichen Itza was designed and built about 1000 years later so, in light of this, the design standards would have changed significantly. I measured whatever steps I could find in the El Mirador region and found that they were usually about 300 mm. I could not make a clear measurement connection. I was looking for 262 mm. No luck here either.

Too much ambiguity. Too many variables. The only conclusion is that I am still without any conclusion.

Image 41: Fresh jaguar footprint in the mud

On the final 10 kilometres of that incredible trek, the elusive jaguar I had been looking for made himself known. A fresh track was imprinted in the mud in front of us. It would have been no more than an hour old. We had crossed paths, and I knew then I had entered into the heartland of this mysterious landscape where I had encountered spirit lights from another world, another time. But as I left El Mirador, it was a yearning for a coffee and a comfortable bed that became the focus of my attention.

Chapter 5 : The Neurotransmitter Fix

Image 42: Temple 1 in Tikal is approximately 47 metres high

The towering edifices at Tikal stood like giant beacons of stone projecting above the treetops. Feeling exhausted by the enormous task ahead of me, I resigned myself to the fact I would probably never have the resources to confirm the use of the measurement system outside of Chichen Itza in Mexico.

Image 43: Sacred Ceiba tree

I met a young couple from Europe on the way to Tikal and spoke to them about my aspirations. They came up with an idea to enlist the support of young travellers to help measure the temples. Crowd measuring was hatched in a bus in northern Guatemala. I wondered if that would work: a whole army of young people measuring the temples. All that data collated into a comprehensive record, which at the end would give a cross-reference of the entire Maya measurement system. I had no idea how to implement such a plan. At the time of writing this, I wonder if it will ever happen, thousands of amateur archaeologists enlisted to help change history.

Image 44: An ocellated turkey

Chapter 5 : The Neurotransmitter Fix

Image 45: Fuego Volcano activity, south-western Guatemala

Serotonin

Just before I left Flores, I was casually chatting with the cleaner in the hotel where I was staying, a young indigenous Maya lady named Maria. I learned she was being made redundant due to the downturn in local tourism during the months of October and November. My heart went out to her as I was told she has no father and supports her mother. She worked hard, and I felt she did not need that, nor deserve it. As soon as she said "no father", my parental responsibility was activated. Right, I said to myself. Before I leave, I am going to help this young lady, who was about 20 years old. She dreams of a better life like all of us. Young women don't get paid very much in this country and are very much disadvantaged—about $7 a day, which is not enough to live on.

The father/parent emotion inside me went to work. I felt a responsibility not to walk away and abandon her, abandoned, once by her father and again by somebody who might be able to help. I moved out of the hotel to a backpacker hostel to save money. There, I asked the owner if he needed someone to work in his new hostel. He did. He was conducting interviews right at that moment. That was synchronicity. I wanted to get this girl through the door no matter what. I offered to pay the first week's wages for her, which was about A$60. (How could he say no to that?) She had the interview and got the job.

This isn't about how nice a guy I am. $60 is not a huge amount in Australia, although it is in Guatemala. This is about a random act of kindness, unconditional, no strings attached. I was interested in how a chance meeting can change the direction of somebody's life. How the unseen forces working behind the scenes nudge us, influence us to act and thereby send someone else down a new pathway. It just felt good to help someone in need. It felt like the right thing to do in the moment.

This event encouraged me to investigate what makes us feel this need to support someone else. I found there is scientific evidence of brain chemicals at work that could be the reason. Our body produces hundreds of neurochemicals, of which only a small fraction have been identified. I went looking for one that relates to the feeling of mental satisfaction and wellbeing, the chemical released that makes us feel good when we do something nice for someone else.

Scientists believe human beings are hardwired to avoid pain and suffering, preferring pleasure instead. I think that is pretty obvious. I choose laughing over crying anytime. A chemical process is at work in the brain that most of us are unaware of. Our brains are physiologically designed to release chemicals into our body that make us feel good. Happiness is influenced by neurotransmitters released by nerve fibres.

One of these brain chemicals is called serotonin. This neurotransmitter circulates in the blood throughout the central nervous system. Scientists also refer to serotonin as the "happiness chemical" because it is linked to mood levels. Another neurotransmitter is dopamine. This chemical influences our ability to concentrate and remember information, as well as helping determine the quality of our sleep. Dopamine is released after a goal is reached. It plays a role in our ability to efficiently organise our lives. Dopamine happiness feels invigorating and energising. The mind knows that an objective has been achieved and will inform our body by flooding it with dopamine, causing us to feel fulfilled, both physically and mentally.

I had a goal of getting Maria a job, and the level of satisfaction I felt when I achieved that sent my dopamine levels soaring.

Essentially, it is a scientific fact we are intrinsically designed to help our fellow human beings because, chemically, it makes us feel good. Naturally, one needs to be able to discriminate between those who really need help and those who are just energy vultures. Maria's father left home when she was eight years old and she has not seen him since.

I went to Guatemala looking for a measurement to back up my mathematical theory. Instead, I discovered the measurement system that determines the quality of human beings is not so much the distance from the fingertips to the elbow. It is in our capacity to help someone else in need. Empathy, compassion, and all those other nice words are really about ourselves in a sense. We are not taught this in school. We are told to sit up straight and behave (and learn mathematics). Why is this proven scientific medical fact about helping someone not part of the education curriculum? I believe it should be. We should be educated, reminded, trained and encouraged to help one another for our own peace of mind from a very young age. It's not just about making ourselves look good to our friends or being socially responsible. It's a scientific truth.

Scientific evidence suggests we are physiologically and psychologically designed to care for each other's wellbeing.

Maria thanked me for finding her that job. What I did for her was small. What she did for me was far greater. She made me more conscious of the science of wellbeing and reminded me this is the way to live. Our chance meeting changed my perception, probably more than it changed her circumstances. Now I am addicted. I have a need for more of these brain chemicals to be activated; I require my serotonin and dopamine substance fix on a continual basis and look for opportunities to get some. I really should be thanking Maria. She is the hero in this story.

If you want success, then pursue success for others. If you want happiness, seek out happiness for someone else. If you want to end your own suffering, then alleviate the suffering of the person next to you. Finally, if it is power and control you need, then give it to the people.

Image 46: Indigenous Maya girl, Maria Ac Pop

Why Maria?

I probably would have walked past hundreds of people who were in a more desperate situation than Maria. So, what was it that prompted me to help her rather than a person going through a rubbish bin looking for food? Not really sure. It just happened. Sometimes I have the ability to instantly recognise potential in people. That has happened on numerous occasions for me and I feel compelled to tell them. I could see in Maria the potential to be a future humanitarian. Perhaps she will be an active voice for the oppressed and underprivileged. By a small act of kindness from me, she may be nudged in that direction. I don't really know. I just have a feeling. This is not about being a rescuer or enabler, as it is called. The circumstances and environment in which she lived required some kind of assistance. As John Travolta once said during a televised news story, upon landing in New Orleans after Hurricane Katrina devastated the region in 2005, "If we have the means, then we have the obligation."

Perhaps this is the way of the future. At the turn of the Maya calendar a new cycle begins, so it is said. To live in the modern world, the new Anthropocene epoch, perhaps the only way to survive will be to live

Chapter 5 : The Neurotransmitter Fix

for the benefit of someone else. Altruism could be the primary method of functioning as the new Maya cycle begins. That is my opinion, my prophecy if you like.

As the bus carried me away from Guatemala, on the way to Palenque in Mexico, I had mixed emotions. I was leaving empty-handed as far as physical evidence to support my research. But that didn't bother me so much because now I had a sense of this mysterious country and its people. I was leaving this land, imbued with a history so profound there are no words, a country of complete contrasts, polarised yet mystical.

Yes, I leave empty-handed as far as my theory goes; however, I leave with my new addiction to brain chemicals, and I take with me a sense of the people—their genuine, warm, open smiles and welcoming faces that break into laughter with ease. Underlying, there is a resolute strength born of thousands of years of adversity. A fertile land where a fertile imagination brought to light the refined, mysterious art of the Maya. I felt at home there. I identified with the psyche of the people like nowhere else on earth I have been, after having travelled to 37 different countries. That for me is, and always will be, Guatemala—the land of the eternal spring.

Image 47: Three little pigs

Image 48: A green-billed toucan reaches for a berry

Last Chance

Entering Mexico, I noticed the plentiful wi-fi I had become accustomed to in Guatemala virtually disappear. In front of me, Palenque finally appeared after a slow and tedious border crossing. It is undoubtedly one of the most strikingly beautiful archaeological sites I have seen on this entire odyssey. Nestled on the side of a mountain, the site clearly displayed the aesthetic vision of its architect and designer, Pakal.

Image 49: Palenque ruins, Mexico

Archaeologists believe Palenque was first occupied around 100 BCE (late Preclassic to early Classic period), which is about four or five hundred years earlier than when Chichen Itza was built. Perhaps there were some philosophical or aesthetic influences in terms of measurement from the same era. Once again, however, every flight of steps was nowhere near the measurement I was looking for. They were irregular and ravaged by time. What stairways I could find that were somewhat straight, I understood had been restored, so I was still without a clear resolution.

Image 50: A design feature in the architecture at Palenque known as a tau cross

I noticed some unusual design features built into the walls. They were in the shape of a T, sometimes known as the tau cross. There is considerable speculation about what exactly they could have meant to the Maya. Why not measure them? Because that is what I do. I measured about seven different ones. Bingo. I was able to tick the final box. The horizontal crossbar was, on average, 524 mm (± 3 mm) in length. That equals one cubit, or two spans, identical to the height of two steps at Chichen Itza.

Image 51: Measuring the tau cross, which equals approximately one cubit

Whether this design measurement was deliberate, I do not know. I may never know, with so much ambiguity surrounding what I was attempting. Should my research at Chichen Itza gain some traction in mainstream academia, it might inspire others to continue the investigation. At the time of writing this book, my research capacity is totally exhausted. Not only that, so am I.

I had already found the evidence in the mathematics of the Temple of Kukulkan. Anything else would have been a bonus. Besides, a geometric secret is already encoded in their oral history as plain as day. It is in the sacred creation text narrative still read by Maya today, the *Popol Vuh*.

> **the fourfold siding, fourfold cornering,
> measuring, fourfold staking,**
> halving the cord, stretching the cord
> in the sky, on the earth,
> **the four sides, the four corners**, as it is said,
> by the Maker, Modeler, ...
> (D. Tedlock, 1996, pp. 63–64, emphasis added)

Chapter 5 : The Neurotransmitter Fix

Image 52: A Chac Mool statue, photographed at Chichen Itza, Mexico

Chapter 6

Temporary Residence

According to the United Nations, more people on earth are on the move now than at any time in history.[1] Political corruption, civil wars and environmental factors are the leading causes of this upheaval. We are now witnessing the highest levels of displacement on record, with 2018 figures revealing an unprecedented 70 million people around the world who have been forced from their homes. This includes nearly 30 million refugees, over half of whom are under the age of 18 (United Nations, n.d.).

Furthermore, millions of stateless people have been denied a nationality and access to basic rights such as education, healthcare, employment and freedom of movement. Almost **every two seconds, one person is forcibly displaced** as a result of conflict or persecution (United Nations, n.d.). Environmental destruction is one of the most recent causes for displacement.

In India, Prime Minister Narendra Modi's ruling Bharatiya Janata Party is preparing to release the final version of a controversial list called the National Register of Citizens (India Today, 2019). This could result in another two million people displaced overnight near its border with Bangladesh. This was in 2019. We are looking at numbers that could be described as biblical proportions.

---

1. *This has changed temporarily at the time of writing as governments around the world have imposed mandatory lockdowns because of the COVID-19 virus.*

Chapter 6 : Temporary Residence

During the time of the attack on Israel thousands of years ago by the Abyssinian king, Nebuchadnezzar II, with the subsequent forced evacuation, those dispersed early settlers were like today's refugees. The only difference is the relative scale in numbers. Not unlike the lost tribes of Israel, the modern-day equivalent experience for so many people is similar to what the ancient Israelis endured thousands of years ago: no place to stop, no place to go. Families were separated without the means to reconnect with loved ones and extended relatives. Perhaps we are just seeing the start of the scale of this human tragedy as climate change becomes irreversible, which the scientists are warning.

In 2019 the US president, Donald Trump, hatched a plan to make Guatemala a safe zone for refugees who were moving from El Salvador and Honduras. A quick look at the demographics of refugees crossing the US border from Mexico shows that most are Guatemalan nationals. This plan demonstrates either a complete lack of understanding on the part of American foreign policy or that there is some other agenda at work behind the scenes.

Displaced people are not necessarily on the move. I say this based on my experience. This land down under, Australia, has been good to me. Rich in natural beauty, resources and wide-open spaces. It was this place that led me to a study of the stars. As a child, the cosmos lighting up the heavens had me up late at night investigating the out-of-reach realms with a telescope. That background has brought me to this stage in my life.

We, as a nation, have been lucky, and I love this country without a doubt. From all over the world, people want to come here to Australia because they see this place as the land of opportunity. This is largely due to our isolation and, therefore, a lack of neighbours on our doorstep sharing our border. As comedian John Cleese once joked, there are planets closer to earth than Australia is to other countries. Here, we have freedom of expression and freedom of movement. Just how long that will last remains to be seen.

Australians are blunt and sometimes crude. I love that about us. But that characteristic is not always palatable for some people from overseas. Sometimes we have no filter. There is a certain freedom in that. What is on the mind comes out through the mouth. Whoops, perhaps I should not have said that. Oh well, too late. Better out than in. (There is a price to pay, for what you say.)

Yet, all this said and done, I feel I have more of an affinity with the land across the Pacific Ocean that was once the Maya stronghold, Guatemala. It felt right to be there. I had remembered my way back to a place where I felt connected. In this context, I feel I am a member of one of the lost tribes who, over the generations, somehow lost contact with the past. In Australia, I feel at home but not totally at rest. A temporary resident in a foreign land. I appreciate the safety and the lifestyle. I value so many things about Australia. However, I seem predisposed to think like a Mayan. I walk like a Mayan. My stature is Mayan and I have an affinity with their concepts, their art and their architecture. When I am not there, I have a sense of longing to go back. Peace of mind, for me, is not having that feeling of needing to be somewhere else.

I suspect many people around the world feel like this: living in their country of birth, but not at rest—a feeling of not being totally in tune with the local psyche. At home and yet somehow spiritually disconnected, trying to remember where they belong. Adding the physically displaced people together with the spiritually disconnected, 70 million may just be the tip of the iceberg.

The displaced people of today might also be called the lost tribes. Do all of us feel we are on earth in the wrong place, at the right time? If we all were able to go freely where we think we belong, then would the world change? A world without territorial borders where circumstances do not impede movement. A world where everyone is where they ought to be, where they should be, to be truly free without social conditioning or national restrictions. If we could just remember where that place is. Would that end the conflict that is characteristic of the human condition?

If everyone found their tribe, their connection to place, to the land, would contentment return to earth, to the proverbial Garden of Eden? Would the lost be found? Would the Messiah be made redundant?

Inflicted Conflict

Guatemala is experiencing transmigration and dislocation of its people at unprecedented levels. Demographic data about those apprehended at the US border shows the number of Guatemalans dispossessed from their home has risen from approximately 20,000 in 2007 to over 115,000 in 2017 (Cohn, Passel, & Gonzalez-Barrera, 2017). The entire history of the Maya of Mesoamerica, even before the conquest by the Spanish, is punctuated with conflict.

Civil conflict

Archaeologists believe the Maya had to defend themselves from various neighbouring tribes. Bonampak is an ancient Maya archaeological site, known for its murals, in the Mexican state of Chiapas near the border with Guatemala. It is approximately 30 km south of the larger site of Yaxchilan. The construction of the site dates to around the late Classic period (c. 580–800 CE). The murals depict what appears to be a war scene where the captives met their unfortunate demise at the hands of the victors, decapitation. This depiction of war events is not altogether different from how military battles are remembered today, such as the Australian experience with the Battle of Gallipoli in World War I, commemorated annually through Anzac Day and on memorials throughout the country.

The culture of human sacrifice of ancient Mesoamerica has its modern-day equivalents. It is not that far removed from a suicide bomber who walks into a crowded restaurant and blows themselves and everyone around them into oblivion. Or a soldier who runs onto a battlefield, knowing the odds of survival are minimal. Essentially, it is about surrendering one's life for a perceived greater cause. Although hardly recognised as such, human sacrifice is disguised in all sorts of so-called noble aspirations and is very much a contemporary occurrence. The Maya could have been assertively defending their intellectual copyright.

When the Spanish arrived in Mesoamerica in the 1500s, the civilisation as a whole was already significantly reduced in size. The temples were mostly abandoned. Some researchers believe this was the result of environmental damage caused by deforestation. It took considerable timber resources to produce the limestone mortar for construction of the large temples such as those at Tikal and El Mirador in Guatemala and Chichen Itza in Mexico. There is also evidence that drought influenced their demise. As a result of scarce resources, there would have been infighting among the people. The scarcity of natural resources between neighbouring groups may have been a contentious issue leading to conflict back then as it does now.

Foreign exploitation

The term "banana republic" was born in Guatemala. This was due to the influence of a powerful American organisation called the United Fruit Company. Formed in 1899, it had a significant impact on the development of Latin American countries. The company owned considerable property in the Caribbean lowlands, having a high degree of control over transportation networks such as railways and steamships. With laws in place supporting individuals in a corrupt government, the company was able to expand throughout the region. Its profits benefited overseas investors instead of local Guatemalans. It has been suggested the United Fruit Company was responsible for severe environmental degradation and loss of biodiversity through its farming techniques (Putnam, 2002).

Genocide

More recently, the Maya have suffered at the hands of their fellow citizens. This injustice is referred to as the Silent Genocide. Since 1980, the Guatemalan military has allegedly caused the deaths of around 45,000 to 60,000 adults. Some allege this campaign was backed by the US Central Intelligence Agency (CIA, n.d.). To this day, there have been few convictions, and it stands as one of the world's worst examples of crimes against humanity. Individuals believed to be responsible within the Guatemalan military have largely gone unpunished. Families are still fighting for justice. The Silent Genocide is a subject hardly anyone wants to talk about and hardly anyone outside the country knows about.

Climate change

In 2020 we again see evidence of environmental influences and government corruption fragmenting the remaining population and causing the disassembling of their cultural practices. Guatemala is listed as one of the top 10 countries to be directly affected by climate change (Steffens, 2018). A prolonged drought has brought this ancient society to its knees, with many Maya forced to relocate from their traditional farming regions to the urban areas of Guatemala City. History repeats itself. Whatever the reason for the original demise of the Maya civilisation, it is happening again as the burden of climate change is added to the shoulders of an already weary population.

Cultural exodus

Most of today's Guatemalans are direct descendants of a once-great civilisation. There are about 7 million Maya, some of whom choose to speak their own language and no other. Perhaps this is in defiance of the Spanish conquest, a lingering resentment from the past.

I wondered if these people could access more easily than others the brain-wired mechanism for developing skills in sciences such as astrophysics, geometry and mathematics, as their ancestors had before them. Would it be easier for them to excel, within the scope of their ancestral lineage, due to a predisposition and innate ability? Perhaps, through the cognitive process of remembering, this could be the key to opening the door and thereby accessing the scientific knowledge and mystical wisdom of their ancestors.

While living with the experience of poverty, not many opportunities exist to get scientifically or spiritually educated on the road to America. There is not much time left, after trying to survive, to remember the wisdom from the past. It would be difficult to focus on higher levels of thought when the basic need to just get enough food for the day preoccupies the mind.

I thought about this as I learned how the Maya people in Guatemala, in many cases, are looked down upon as almost second-class citizens in their own country. What a contradiction. Although comprising over 40%

of the population, they are the most disadvantaged people in the country. What is the world missing out on in terms of science and art as the descendants of one of the most scientifically and intellectually advanced ancient civilisations on earth are continually brought to their knees? The wall between Mexico and the USA proposed by the US president, Donald Trump, is like another nail in their coffin. By our inaction, are we all the passive Nebuchadnezzars of the new millennium? Collectively, we should be embarrassed to allow this to happen to the people who are descendants of such a magnificent civilisation.

My travel toward the Mexican border coincided with planned protests across the country against an allegedly corrupt Guatemalan Government. The people live under a system that allows immunity for those in government. In other words, one law for the politicians, one for the people. Well, of course, that will cause resentment among the people.

It was Columbus Day on 12 October 2019. The Maya had staged a protest at Tikal. As a friend of mine commented, this event never made the local newspapers or media. The indigenous Maya see the arrival of Columbus as the day that started the invasion and the attempted destruction of their culture. This is similar to Indigenous Australians with regard to the arrival of the First Fleet in 1788. In the USA, Columbus Day is a reason to celebrate: polarised viewpoints, polarised perspectives.

I feel that this civilisation, the Maya, needs the world's assistance now more than ever. It is devastating for me to know they have to leave their country in order to survive. This is not just about them. It is about the survival of the whole world and the inarguably perilous, dislocated position we have found ourselves in. I am not suggesting we revert to human sacrifice and tribal living. It is the mystical, spiritual connection to the cosmos that is missing in governments, cultures and societies of the world today. Perhaps technology and spirituality can coexist.

More than ever, humanity needs the Maya to regroup and become the fantastic civilisation they once were.

Chapter 6 : Temporary Residence

*Image 53: Maya ceremony at Tikal, Guatemala
(photograph by Jerson Gonzalez)*

Chapter 7

Under a Starless Sky

Do not take roads travelled by the public.
—Pythagoras (ca. 570–495 BCE)

On New Year's Eve 2019, I set foot on the *Phoenicia* once again after it had arrived in the Dominican Republic from Tunisia. The mission was accomplished on the part of Captain Philip Beale and his crew as they all participated in challenging the historical records regarding contact with pre-Columbian America. The New Year fireworks lit up the night sky. With the ship's arrival, a light was shone on a lost part of history. They had proven that a vessel built to technically identical standards as that constructed in 600 BCE could successfully cross the Atlantic Ocean. The journey was accomplished in just 39 days.

Chapter 7 : Under a Starless Sky

*Image 54: The arrival of the **Phoenicia** in the Dominican Republic after crossing the Atlantic Ocean*

Map 5: The journey of the Phoenicia from Tunisia to the Dominican Republic and on to Miami, Florida, USA

The Unexpected Zodiac

Not unlike my trip through Guatemala, I came here to this country in search of evidence to back up my theory that a unit of measurement could have made its way across the Atlantic Ocean thousands of years ago. I believe it may have arrived in the New World by means of a ship like the *Phoenicia*. By a stroke of luck, I had managed get myself on board as part of the crew to finish the final leg to the USA.

I propose that by some remarkable sequence of events, there was a collaboration between two ancient civilisations. The unit of measurement, the cubit, along with the six-pointed star, is very much characteristic of the Mediterranean region. The timeframes from the Maya calendar are specifically Mesoamerican. The Temple of Kukulkan holds these two fundamental principles of design clearly within its construction. If the ancient Phoenicians had made it here, to the Dominican Republic, then that would be historically significant and supportive of my theory of how the unit of measurement may have arrived in Mesoamerica.

The new year had begun. Throughout the capital city, Santo Domingo, there was dancing in the streets. In DR, as it is known locally, there is always an excuse to move with the music. These people have a predisposition toward celebrating life even though there is extreme poverty without adequate social services. Like most countries around the world, the very rich live alongside the extremely poor.

A few days later, on the other side of the world in Iran, an explosion also lit up the night sky after a Ukrainian airliner was accidentally shot down. This incident, attributed to human error, occurred directly after the US president, Donald Trump, ordered the assassination of an Iranian military general, Qasem Soleimani. America had set the tone for the Middle East, perhaps for decades to come. Extrajudicial killing without the process of trial is the favoured option now as it saves a lot of time and money wasted on the legal process. Get the job done. The silence is deafening on the part of world leaders.

The Dominican Republic is on the eastern side of an island called Hispaniola that is separated into two nations. To the west is the small country of Haiti. It was here, in Hispaniola, where Christopher Columbus established a base and to which he returned a total of four times. He suggested this may have been the location of the fabled biblical place called Ophir.

Ophir, an elusive place recorded in biblical text, is a location where there was thought to be abundant riches. King Solomon needed money to finance his temple. He ordered the construction of a fleet of vessels to voyage to foreign lands in search of riches. Ophir became a destination presumably known only to those who went there and returned. Historians argue about its exact location. India stands as a likely possibility as well as Africa. My intuitive interpretation is that Ophir is more likely the term used to describe the expedition holistically rather than a name assigned to a specific location. Over a three-year expedition period, it is logical to assume the vessels would have visited many places where they gathered various things they deemed to have value. One of those places may have been Hispaniola.

I spoke to Captain Beale about this possibility. He surmised Columbus may have used Ophir as leverage to influence King Ferdinand and Queen Isabella of Spain to fund his voyage. Perhaps King Solomon and King Ferdinand had the same agenda—wealth. Eventually, the exploration of the rest of Central America proved lucrative for the Spanish with the ransacking of gold from various civilisations on the mainland.

Ophir is a journey, not a destination.

At about the same time, in around 600 BCE, an Egyptian pharaoh, Necho II, called for a fleet to be built to circumnavigate the African continent then known as Libya. A reference to this journey was recorded by the Greek historian Herodotus in 440 BCE (Krüger, 2014). The fleet was operated by Phoenicians because it was these people who were considered the most capable of undertaking such a journey and returning safely.

In 2009, Captain Philip Beale and his crew sailed around Africa in the *Phoenicia*. He did this not only to prove the Phoenicians were capable of achieving the task set by Pharaoh Necho II, but also to suggest they were probably the most advanced seafarers of their time. About 10 years later, after traversing the earth for well over 20,000 nautical miles, the *Phoenicia* made its successful voyage across the Atlantic Ocean to the

Dominican Republic where it is believed Christopher Columbus arrived on one of his first expeditions.

During this epic journey across the Atlantic Ocean from Tunisia, Captain Beale and his crew were greeted by the Lebanese community at various ports. The Lebanese are striving to establish the rightful contribution to the world made by the Phoenicians. Lebanon is the country that now occupies ancient Phoenician land bordering Israel. Phoenicians were a Semitic-speaking civilisation based specifically in Lebanon, Syria and northern Palestine. Lebanese people see the Phoenicians as an integral part of their ancestral heritage.

Christopher Columbus is famous for discovering the Americas, although he never actually set foot on US soil. He only made it to the Caribbean. His reputation is somewhat tainted as records indicate his treatment of the native population was harsh. Although it is believed numerous natives died of sickness and disease due to a lack of immunity to the foreigners, many more died as a result of torture and murder. Some members of the Jewish community hold Columbus in high esteem as they see him as the one who found a land where they are finally not forced to move on, as has been their experience in other parts of the world. Some writers, like Nazi hunter Simon Wiesenthal in his book *Sails of Hope* (1973), argue Columbus may have been of Jewish background (Borschel-Dan, 2018). I wondered if he was secretly looking for evidence of the lost tribes.

The arrival of the Italian navigator and his Spanish crew on Hispaniola meant complete disaster for the local indigenous people known as the Taíno. They were an Arawak-speaking people who are believed to have arrived from the mainland of Central America. After surviving thousands of years, they are now, with a little help from the Spanish conquerors, virtually extinct or have been absorbed into the community. It is believed that the Maya from the mainland traded with the local indigenous Taíno people. Christopher Columbus encountered the Maya on his fourth voyage in 1502. In a detailed account, he described the Maya vessel:

> There arrived at that time a canoe long as a galley and 8 feet [2.5 m] wide, made of a single tree trunk like the other Indian canoes: it was freighted with merchandise ... Amidships it

had a palm-leaf awning … Under this awning were the children and women and all the baggage and merchandise … There were twenty-five paddlers aboard, but they offered no resistance. (Keen, 1959, as cited in Peck, 2005, pp. 117–118)

Image 55: Columbus may have had an affection for pigeons, yet he developed a strong dislike for the local Taíno population

Physical evidence of Phoenician contact with the Dominican Republic remains anecdotal, to say the least. Some crew members of the *Phoenicia* and I were looking high and low for a connection. I talked with anthropologists and local historians; however, nothing conclusive surfaced. If there remained some strong evidence of architectural ruins dating before the pre-Columbian era, I would be inclined to measure them and therefore form an evidence-based opinion. In saying this, I do not discount the strong possibility of contact.

What struck me as remarkable was the speed with which the Spanish colonised the Dominican Republic. Columbus first arrived in 1492. Less than 25 years later, in 1514, construction began on the Cathedral of Santa María la Menor. It is believed to be one of the first churches in the New World. Another of the oldest buildings in the Americas is the Dominican Convent. Its construction began even earlier with the arrival of the Dominican Order around 1510. In a vaulted ceiling, a legacy of the masonic order of Freemasons remains frozen in architecture where the 12 zodiac signs are depicted (Image 56).

Image 56: Domed ceiling in the Dominican Convent with 32 rays emanating from the centre, most likely representing the 32nd degree of the Masonic order

The Freemason movement links its heritage to ancient mystical schools of thought, describing its foundation as having originated in ancient Phoenicia. The movement holds Hiram Abiff, the chief architect of Solomon's Temple, to be the first Freemason. This underpins the third degree of the Masonic order. So, in a sense, and in this context, the Phoenicians did make their way to the Dominican Republic. Their understanding of mathematics and geometry reached out across the centuries by way of influencing the Freemasons, who it appears were involved with the design and construction of the Dominican Convent.

Chapter 7 : Under a Starless Sky

The *Phoenicia* made it across the Atlantic Ocean in just 39 days, so that in itself is strong evidence foreign contact with the Caribbean was possible before Columbus.

A prominent person from ancient history has direct links to the Phoenicians: Pythagoras, the mathematician and philosopher. Although he was born on the Greek island of Samos in about 570 BCE, his father was a Phoenician merchant. Therefore, it could be argued that he has stronger links to the Phoenician civilisation than to ancient Greece. Not only has much of Phoenician history been obscured by the centuries, but they have also often been robbed of their connection with one of the greatest mathematicians and philosophers from ancient history.

The pathways of Santo Domingo have been walked by many famous people. Apart from Columbus, the English naval captain Sir Francis Drake left his fingerprints by way of cannon-fire attacks on some of the churches. This was known as the Battle of Santo Domingo in 1586 (Kraus, 1970). Violence and civil conflict pervade the historical landscape of Hispaniola.

Image 57: Sunset over the Caribbean

*Image 58: The sails of the **Phoenicia***

Dementia on the Caribbean

As the Dominican Republic slipped away under the waves, it felt to me the *Phoenicia* was breaking into a gallop even though it was only doing 5 knots. The solid mass of terra firma rapidly dissolved into liquid. She was in a hurry to get somewhere and the excitement level rose to meet the wind in the sails. A flying fish flew straight through the window of the cabin, landing on the kitchen floor. I am on board a floating sushi restaurant. The flying fish soon became a frying fish. I photographed another type of fish becoming airborne, presumably trying to escape a predator from the ocean depths. It was then confronted by two more winged predators from the air. Fly, fish fly! Is there really any rest for any of us, any living creature inhabiting a body comprised of flesh and bone?

Chapter 7 : Under a Starless Sky

The *Phoenicia* is a one-off. It is highly unlikely anyone will ever build a vessel identical to this again. A voyage like this has not been done for the last 2000 years or so and probably will never be repeated. I considered myself fortunate to be one of the few people who have had the opportunity to participate in a once-in-a-lifetime experience. It fits perfectly with my theory of foreign contact with pre-Columbian Mesoamerica.

People are drawn to the *Phoenicia* because they recognise its unique qualities. There is a certain energy about it. They are lured by its distinct magnetic ambience. It is confronting for many visitors when they imagine themselves involved and how they would function if they were on board for an extended period. The lack of comfort and personal privacy, and the physical difficulty, would be far too challenging, as many people expressed.

The options for going to the toilet are limited. However, that is something that just cannot be avoided. It is either eventually go in full public view, or the other option is … well, there isn't one. Some biological functions have no concern for social etiquette. Some things just have to be done regardless of the environment. The best I can do is postpone the inevitable for as long as possible. After a while, though, it doesn't matter who is watching. In fact, if I happen to glance in that general direction at an inappropriate moment, the image of strained facial expressions is something I want to delete from my memory as soon as possible. I presume that is the same for anyone. I nicknamed it "the loo with a view". We washed our clothes in salt water and hoped rain would rinse them, as fresh water is a valuable resource.

Image 59: The toilet

We were a crew made up of multiple nationalities: two Brazilians, a Lebanese, one from the Netherlands, an Indonesian, two people from England and another two from Norway. Three out of the 10 crew in total were female. I thought I spoke English perfectly; however, most things I said often had to be repeated. Australian English is indiscernible from babbling to the ear of many nationalities. I had lots of good laughs on this trip with some of the crew. Thankfully they were all capable sailors. My experience at sea was limited, to say the least; however, I had about two weeks' worth of jokes, which seemed to have the desired effect, but not always. If the trip went on too long, I would have to start repeating my jokes in the hope the others had forgotten them. It didn't work. Humour is subjective; however, my Australian accent was a source of amusement for some. There was one thing we all had in common—we all loved the *Phoenicia*.

There are a few social mores on board that don't exist anywhere else. One absolute no-no is to wash someone else's cup. They become individual hand-crafted items over many consecutive meals. The greater the build-up of coffee and tea stains on the inside surface, the better the next one tastes.

Chapter 7 : Under a Starless Sky

I listened to the Eagles' song "Hotel California" on somebody's playlist regularly, under the vault of the heavens sprinkled by a never-ending array of stars. This shouldn't be too hard taking this project on, I thought to myself. After all, I had survived a 91-kilometre trek through the Guatemalan jungle just a few months prior. However, unforeseen surprises were in store for me.

I get my energy from being alone. But being an introvert is not always an advantage. Sometimes I just have to get away from people so I can collect my thoughts and regain my composure. I like people but, when they get too much for me, I have to escape. Extroverts need people to get their energy, whereas introverts can function happily without the need for socialising. My predisposition to be alone is certainly an advantage when it comes to being a writer, which sometimes requires isolation for extended periods. The entire publishing budget of this book has probably been spent several times over while sitting alone in various coffee shops.

I knew before I arrived about the dynamics of being on a ship where there is nowhere to escape. Still, I had put myself here for the experience and for the adventure, to be a part of what I believe to be a major historical event. Even though I didn't cross the entire Atlantic Ocean, this last 1600-kilometre leg of the journey from the Dominican Republic to Florida would surely provide sufficient material in terms of research. A 10-day trip was in front of us without contact with the outside world. I was aiming for alternative content to write about rather than grappling with more mathematics and geometry. A little bit of uncomplicated light reading that nobody has to think too hard about to comprehend should fit in here. Perhaps something about pre-Columbian history that is safely removed from me personally would do nicely. Well, sorry, I am a complicated person and complications seem to follow me wherever I go.

A 360-degree horizon has an interesting effect on the mind. I am at the centre of a circular horizon. My conscious memory of family and the people I know and love recedes with the disappearing landscape. There is nothing to distract me from the present. Time has lost its relevance. The only thing that changes is the sea and the sky. The perspective is neither heliocentric nor geocentric. A better description is anthropocentric. People talk in clichés about the benefits of being "in the now" or "living in the moment", yet a strange sense of loss goes with that. That is my experience. Everyone I know is difficult to recall, their voices distant and blurred. The more I am in the present, the more my memory of them fades. That is both intriguing and yet somewhat disturbing. I want to be in the moment, but the last thing I need is to forget my family and the people who have helped fashion who I am. To hold on to all the beautiful moments of my time with them is as much a priority. They should be stored in some easily accessible part of my mind and never ever lose vivid mental contact. I need to know my children are safe.

Are they real? Were they ever real?

My memories are who I am. I am the culmination of my past. The unrealised potential of my future has its foundation back there, behind me. The "now" flashes before my eyes as translucent shadows; the future, a blurred multiple-choice scenario. Without a recollection of the past, I am an empty ship without a rudder, adrift on the vast unending ocean of consciousness. There is no current beneath me, no anchor to connect me, no wind to propel me. I am navigating along the edge of the world under a starless sky.

Image 60: Captain Philip Beale at the helm on board the **Phoenicia**

There were 10 people on board. The roster system was to have one person always at the helm, with another on watch to avoid collision with other vessels at sea. A third was responsible for the bilge pump, while another two took care of the cooking and cleaning. It took five people to operate the ship while the others grabbed as much valuable sleep as the environment would allow. This was done in four-hour and six-hour increments; there was never a full eight hours of solid sleep. As the days passed, I realised a strange thing about myself: I could decipher a 1600-year-old temple more easily than follow a simple roster, which almost proved impossible. I could never tell who was next in the order of assigned work. *How weird is this?*

Beneath the deck was an array of hammocks with the alternative option of sleeping on the floor. One crew member, who had been on a previous leg in a Mediterranean storm, said he did a complete 360-degree rotation in the hammock and never fell out. I cannot imagine how that is possible.

Image 61: Below deck in the sleeping quarters

I have spent only a short time on sailing ships before, and that was 25 years earlier when I was young and indestructible. With age, my balance has diminished somewhat. However, I am here to combat fear. I will not surrender to that emotional state. I will not get old and anxious. This I have told myself time and time again over the last few decades. But that affirmation somehow slips my mind a short time after I hop on the *Phoenicia*. I begin to feel somewhat dislocated. An out-of-body experience is my best description. Separated from a familiar environment, I am in an alien landscape mentally. I had previously asked the universe for adventure and challenge, which is what I yearn for. It is what drives me on. I don't remember asking for memory loss.

I wanted to live on the edge, but out here, everything had suddenly turned back-to-front. When I was on deck, I could see we were heading in one direction by the position of the sun, and yet, as soon as I entered the cabin, the boat had done a complete 180-degree turn. I was facing the opposite way. If there was land to the starboard side on deck, as I took two steps down into the cabin, that same landmass vanished from the view out the cabin window where it should have been. It was relocated on the opposite side. Perhaps the earth had suddenly done an inversion of the poles. North was south. East was west. That was the beginning of my disorientation. The front was at the back and the back was at the front. I have never felt this sensation before. I have always known where north is instinctively. I am from the land down under. This was on the other side of the equator. What a peculiar sensation, somehow lost at sea. No, I am all at sea.

Medically speaking, sleeping in a hammock on board a ship increases the effects of the rocking motion. The *Phoenicia* rocked with the slightest wave, as it had no keel. Blood rushes to the head and then away just as rapidly. According to the ship's doctor, in sleep mode, this is happening continuously. Together with sleep deprivation leading to fatigue, this provides for a disembodied, disconcerting mind-space. I had always been somewhat vague and preoccupied well before I got on board. Now, vagueness has suddenly magnified a hundredfold. To me, these are uncharted mental waters. My brainwave patterns are going strange. I have a book to finish with an obligation to the Maya community. If I lose my memory, all that is gone. I suspect I am the only one alive on earth at present who knows about the mathematics in detail. I am probably the only one obsessive enough to carry this out. Hold on. Hold on.

Chapter 7 : Under a Starless Sky

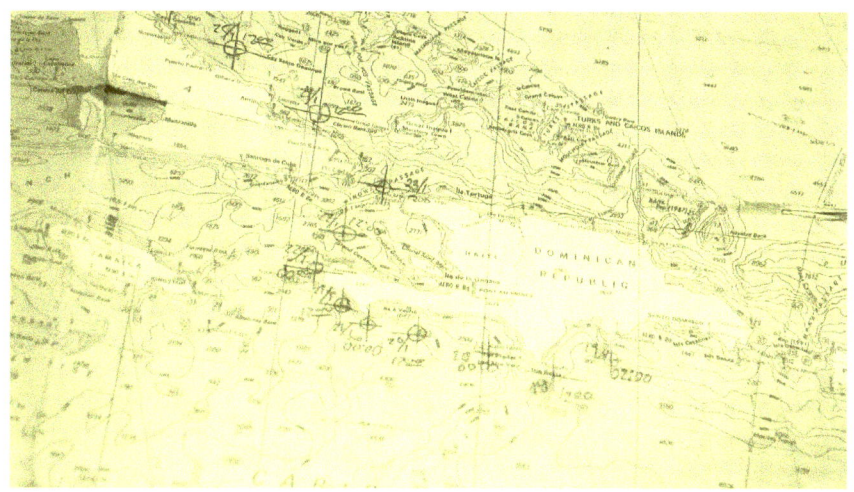

Image 62: Chart showing the way through the Windward Passage

As we round the western Haitian side of the island of Hispaniola, I glance at the map. I see the passageway between Haiti and Cuba called the Windward Passage. A current runs through it like an arterial blood vessel. To me, it resembles a birth canal. I wonder what is in store for us here. It is on the same line of latitude as the Temple of Kukulkan. A storm begins building to the north of us as we approach this relatively narrow passageway. I tend to be sensitive to the influences around me. This could be great fodder for artistic inspiration; however, producing art is the furthest thing from my mind. To add to my imagination, I perceive this area as an entrance to the Bermuda Triangle, the place where things and people go missing.

The environment transforms suddenly as the ocean around us becomes a sea of whitecaps. Everything that isn't nailed or tied down tosses around the cabin as though we are in a clothes dryer. It is hard physical work to hang on to avoid falling over. There is a constant search for something solid to hold, let alone walking from A to B. I suppose this experience is not dissimilar to being in an earthquake. The foundation gives way at every step. Nothing is fixed. All is fluid and in a state of flux. I am weightless one second and heavy the next. Balance is gone and the basics like walking have to be relearned. I am a two-year-old in a grown-up's body.

Image 63: A storm gathers

This is my first storm while on the *Phoenicia*. For me, it rapidly turns into a mental hurricane. The dark of night is upon us. The others had just crossed the Mediterranean and the Atlantic Ocean and are now experienced sailors. My Norwegian sailor companions, one of whom is a Viking tour guide in his homeland, take it in their stride. In fact, everyone takes it in their stride except for me, it seems. I am in personal uncharted waters, the newbie on board. Having an adventure has suddenly moved off my "to-do" list.

At about one o'clock in the morning, a touch of seasickness takes hold. An attractive escape mechanism was to curl up in the fetal position and die. Fatigue forces me to sit for a while, where I quickly doze off. Something catches the release valve on my safety vest, which makes it suddenly inflate automatically. Within seconds, together with a disturbing loud gush of air, I am given a violent bear hug by this expanding plastic thing around my neck. For a moment I think I am being swallowed by an exotic orange marine creature. My sense of humour evaporates.

I learn something about myself on this journey that I sort of know already. I can function as two people simultaneously. I can mow the lawn and study the universe at the same time. I can have all this going on in my

Chapter 7 : Under a Starless Sky

head where the ordinary becomes extraordinary and still manage to continue as though I am not having difficulty functioning. This is the source of my preoccupation. It is better to have physical work to do to keep the mind occupied so I can concentrate on something else and stop thinking about strange things. I never miss a shift, even with the extreme disorientation I am experiencing. There is nowhere to hide, and not revealing yourself is sometimes impossible. This is an extended hypnopompic state of mind somewhere between wide awake and sound asleep.

Someone else arrived on board the *Phoenicia*, uninvited. She is invisible and nobody except me knows she is there. This person is not recorded on the ship's manifest. I have the distinct feeling my mother has arrived.

She had died several years earlier. I sense it is her by the strange thought patterns I am experiencing. I am getting the sensation of a sudden and rapid onset of dementia. I promise myself I will get medically tested should I survive this journey. Recalling things that happened a few moments earlier is near impossible. I know I have a mild case of dyslexia, but this is becoming ridiculous. I cannot follow a simple roster system without assistance. I feel she has arrived and has brought her battle with dementia to the *Phoenicia*. She has lent it to me. Perhaps it is her way of telling me she is here. She is out of her body and comes into mine. But where am I? I am somewhere else.

The sound of the ship leaving the water and crashing into the waves is thunderous. Boom ... boom ... boom! This is magnified below deck. How can a wooden boat take this kind of abuse? She is built as strong as an ox, but being totally waterproof is not one of her attributes. Water finds its way into the sleeping area from every accessible crevice. The smallest crack between the Mediterranean cedar becomes an opportunity for entering below deck without permission. We are invaded by a thousand tiny streams. Mercurial saltwater snakes infiltrate our domain determined to devour the *Phoenicia*, returning it and all of us back to a liquid state.

I begin to understand fully how my mother felt as dementia began to take hold of her mind in her final years. She became infant-like. Sometimes it was difficult not to talk to her as though she was a child. I stopped myself, but it required continual self-monitoring of the way I was communicating. She did not know where to be, what to do, who was who. No more self-determination. Waiting to be told.

I feel as though I embody her experience for a short time. Paranormal activity is not new to me. Was it she who pulled the release tag on my safety vest? I wonder. What is she doing in my body? She has entered my auric field somehow. A walk-in. I know it isn't me in my body for a brief time in that boat during the storm, but where I am, I do not know.

I am now able to fully empathise with her pain, her experience with dementia, and anyone else with the same symptoms for that matter. Before, I was just sympathetic. Now I am empathetic. There is a vast difference between these two emotions.

Finally, the hammock is in sight as my shift ends in the early hours before dawn. To be horizontal is a relief even with the foreseeable incessant rocking on the four-way pivotal axis. I am definitely over having an adventurous lifestyle. But wait, there's more. It doesn't end there. I have a brief moment where I enter another unfamiliar state. With hands across my chest, the thought occurs to me for a split second, this is what I'd look like dead. This is me, gone. A goner. This is another entirely new experience. A state of complete inertia where all is solid and unmoving. I quickly force myself out of that mind frame. That is not a place I need to be. Death by osmosis. No! I will survive this.

Then sleep takes me to another faraway place. I drift into the dreamscape. Once asleep, I enter another out-of-body experience. But this one I am familiar with, having done it before many times. Into the nebulous world I go without concern for my physical body. Dead to the world ... again. Thousands of water snakes have free rein to absorb me into the complexity of their universe. I don't care.

Next day, as the waters calm, we all surface from the damp and musky cavern below deck to a clear blue sky. I am comforted by the fact I am not the only one with a story to tell. One woman says she woke up crying. Another crew member tells me he felt a field of light surround him as he held the helm. Someone else saw the white crest of a wave coming. This was on the descent down from the previous wave. I learn that a 4- or 5-metre single wave had confronted the *Phoenicia* and completely

Chapter 7 : Under a Starless Sky

submerged the horse's head mounted on the bow. I keep my experience mostly to myself. There is a time and place.

Perhaps none of us fully realised how close we came to an NDE (near-death experience). It was somehow real for me. We were almost at one with the Caribbean. The storm had lasted about 12 hours. We all had entered through a gateway into another place using our own individual perception of reality. The doorway into the Bermuda Triangle was ajar. Enter, a 2600-year-old replica sailing ship, the *Phoenicia*, into the place of time warps, disappearances and strange happenings.

Looking back on this, I sometimes wonder why I cannot just experience a simple storm at sea without having all these difficult emotions and feelings to confront. Does everything have to be so bloody intense? But that is me. I am complex and analytical, a dreamer. It is what makes me who I am. It is these aspects of my make-up that allow me to interpret the ancient design of a Maya pyramid built over a thousand years ago. My brain is hardwired that way. This predisposition for the bizarre is inside me. Like most people, a little bit psychic, a little bit clairvoyant. Perhaps, a little bit peculiar. It is the way I am engineered, functioning best in the imaginary world of mysticism and symbolism, the bridge between religion and science. I am who I am. I know who I am … for now.

The rest of the journey to Miami was serene by comparison. The mind wandered between "I am ready for this to end now" to "I want this to go on forever". An occasional whale hugged the starboard side with Cuba off to the port, or was it the other way around? Philosophical conversations as old as humanity evolved about life, freedom and truth, and how the truth is generally avoided. Where is true freedom? What is truth anyway?

With the calming of the ocean, my sense of humour returns, and throughout the rest of the journey I use up my remaining jokes. Then I have to leave. The coronavirus pandemic has started its spread across the world as I fly back to Australia. Beneath me is Trump's America, glimpsed occasionally through the storm clouds. This part of my incredible journey is over, but the memory of being forgetful remains vivid and stark.

The experience of dementia has visited me briefly, either via my mother, someone else, or perhaps as a result of physiological brainwave patterns affected by a bit of sleep deprivation. Believe me, it is not a walk in the park. As I set foot on the coast of Florida, my sojourn into this cruel disease thankfully remained out to sea. But I have had the sensation. Now I can fully empathise with someone going through dementia. It is this aspect of the human condition, empathy, that keeps the human species alive, possibly more than love. With love, comes want and sometimes desire. Empathy is what binds us. It is a type of out-of-body experience where there is total emotional union with someone else. Love in its purest form.

From across the distant horizon … from beyond the Great Divide, the message is this:

Without empathy, humanity is an empty ship without a rudder, adrift on the vast unending ocean of consciousness. There is no current beneath us, no anchor to connect us, no wind to sustain us. Without empathy, we, as a species, are navigating along the edge of the world under a starless sky.

Chapter 8

Remembering, Not Analysing

There's a certain spiritual nature and something of the mind that we can't measure. We can't find it. With all of our sophisticated equipment, we cannot monitor or define it, and yet it's there.
—Ben Carson (2008)

Two years ago, publishing the content of this book would have been totally beyond my capacity. Now, all of a sudden, I have over 50,000 words, together with credible, accurate mathematical equations and diagrams on the architectural design of a 1600-year-old temple. Once I began writing, it seemed to bump along quite rapidly. It was as though I started remembering rather than analysing. But a persistent, intriguing and somewhat perplexing issue for me during this whole roller-coaster ride was how on earth I came upon this thing in the first place. It seemed so obvious to me that what I found was mathematically perfect and beyond argument, but where did it come from? I have been described as having a creative imagination, but I feel I cannot really take the credit for this. I am not that smart.

This odyssey continues, but not on an earthly physical plane. The calculator has been turned off. I have stopped adding and multiplying to venture off exploring the metaphysical. If I had actually time travelled then I want to be able to do it again, this time consciously. I could go off into the future and bring back a cure for cancer or invent something cool like a toaster and get the credit for it. If I had really previously lived in the time of the Maya and can prove it scientifically, then what does that do for science? What does that do for religion? More than that, what does it do for the entire human condition?

Well, I think I have already proven it mathematically, but I'm not sure how to describe what brought this information about. I have the results, but not yet the right name for the experience. I don't have any techniques to share about how to repeat the process, so the scientific method is challenged for this experiment. I don't meditate or practice yoga either, so that rules them out.

In order to rest my mind somehow, the next phase of this journey is about the search for a resolution. This became a trip into the internal landscape of the mind. I began with my own research into independent investigative studies of our brain and its memory system. This was just to help me prove to myself that I was not going completely crazy, or was it too late for that?

Time Travelling or Remembering?

Was I remembering or had I time travelled? Really, is there a difference?

Considerable research has been done concerning how we receive information, how it is stored and recalled both consciously and unconsciously. I became interested in the possibility that I had extended my own memory to include accessing experiences that were not mine. That is, recalling the memories of people who had lived in another time and place. Is that possible?

Memory is electrical energy. We are all electrical energy. There is electrical energy all around us, between molecules, between each other and surrounding the entire earth. Why not across time? This was the premise upon which I based my search. Time travel by remote control without leaving home was my goal to understand. It is cheaper: no waiting at airports, no travel agents.

Memory is intangible, yet it exists. In our consciousness, images can be reactivated along with taste, smell and sound. In a sense, we can time travel via our memory. We can return to different moments in our lives and recall the faces of loved ones or experiences. We can move through time and space in our imagination. In a split second, we are able to travel backwards in time half a century and then return to the present, one second later. Our memory is as fast as the speed of light, perhaps faster. We don't need to experience physical relocation as is often associated with the concept of time travel. Time travelling using our memory is completely different from moving our molecular structure and having to reconstruct it when we get there. Using shared memory would be a much simpler process to explore history. Moreover, it would not cause any problems as far as the time matrix goes. We are not altering our grandfather's decision-making processes—just a little mind-reading, that's all.

Optimistically, I set off across the landscape of the internet looking for research on this topic. It wasn't long before I found some peripheral evidence. Nothing is new. It is already happening.

We are more than our physical bodies.

There was one thing in the environment on earth that became a problem for early scientists to adapt into their methodology. This was the magnetic field. You cannot see, hear, touch, smell or taste it. Yet there is evidence of its existence. It is proven to exist because we can observe the effects it has in the physical world. Although intangible, we know there is a recognisable force operating beyond the boundaries of a given solid structure.

Some believe the same applies to human anatomy. Surrounding our physicality, there is suggested to be an active energy field. Therefore, traditional medicine is also having to contend with the same problem as early scientists, that of recognising and integrating the concept of invisible energy within its practice. In fact, modern medicine is undergoing a rapid transformation. A relatively new branch of the study of human physiology has evolved to address the issue, a collective movement called complementary medicine. Acupuncture, Reiki and yoga are just some of the disciplines that fall under this study. The concept of chi, the force recognised by Chinese medical practitioners for thousands of years, is not readily accepted by contemporary scientific methodology. At the foundation of these practices is the understanding of an invisible force that can be interacted with, or activated, using various techniques with the patient or client.

The term *biofield* was proposed in 1992 by a committee of practitioners and researchers at the US National Institutes of Health (Rubik et al., 2015). The committee defined biofield as "a massless field (not necessarily electromagnetic) that surrounds and permeates living bodies and affects the body" (Rubik et al., 1995, p. 358). Human energy fields pose some difficulty for medical science, with its usual requirements for observed proof, tried and tested results and to be able to withstand the scrutiny of peer review. They face the same problem as the magnetic field. It cannot be readily observed, touched, smelled or tasted.

Modern physicists, on the other hand, are a little more open-minded, having finally reconciled the problem of invisible energy. They have established that even the space between atoms is not empty. It is filled with electrical fields. That would suggest there is nothing in the universe that is not filled with something. We are all connected.

Our memory is a part of an intangible world that can be as vivid as reality itself. Memory is divided into three different types and stored in different areas of the brain (Queensland Brain Institute, 2018). The three types are as follows:

- explicit memory (things that have happened to you plus general facts and information)
- implicit memory (such as motor memories)
- short-term or working memory.

However, our memory is not just contained in the cerebral areas. There is evidence both the heart and the gut have a type of memory. This is expressed in our language as "a gut feeling" or being "heartbroken". We knew this before science did the research to back it up. Documented evidence shows that some people who have had a heart transplant develop interests that the heart donor had. The gut–brain connection is gaining more scientific attention, suggesting they operate independently and yet are intrinsically connected (Courtney, n.d.). Our body and mind are hardwired to respond to both external and internal stimuli through some sort of interrelated chemical and electrical process.

Futurists predict that a brave new world awaits us: that of being transhuman. This is where the distinguishing lines are blurred between human anatomy and technology. As part of this transition in medicine, understanding the functions of the brain and memory is gaining increasing attention.

Brain–computer interface, or BCI, is just one branch of numerous developments in brain research. This can be simply described as the hypothetical concept of digitally scanning the content of the brain and memory, enabling it to be transferred to a computer. Research is embryonic in its development at the moment; however, there is substantial movement toward it becoming a reality (Shih et al., 2012).

Imagine that, the ability to copy your brain and memory, then upload it to a computer, giving the capacity to email it around the world in a split second. You could do multiple emails. Other people may not be able to distinguish you, the original, from all the other copies. Therefore, the real you may be perceived as just a copy. One of your copies may become radical and claim itself as the original, thereby taking action to delete you permanently. You could even absolve yourself from responsibility by blaming one of your copies for saying something wrong. A brave new world of potential mistaken identity awaits us. All your memories could be uploaded to Facebook, including your bank account passwords for the world to review. Your memories could be stored in a server somewhere and accessed by anyone from the future. Or, referencing the context of the research in this book, you might have built a house using a certain measurement you wanted to keep secret. Then, someone from the future accesses your memory database and works out how you went about it.

Our brain is kept busy processing millions of tasks simultaneously. Because it is part of our biological mechanism, to function it needs to regulate everything that we do unconsciously. If it were relocated to another substrate, like a small computer, it could spend a lot more time doing more important things, like thinking.

Even Elon Musk is entering the race with his brain–machine interface company, Neuralink. I watched his presentation video, where he commented to the live audience: "With a high-bandwidth brain–machine interface, I think we can … go along for the ride and … effectively have the option of merging with AI" (CNET, 2019, 2:49). That inspired me to wonder just how long it will be before it changes from optional to mandatory. An individual may one day be influenced or coerced into making that dramatic decision. Will the day come when everyone is forced to do it? Whoever is watching a small portion of our lives now will be able to watch everything, including our entire historical memory.

All sorts of people are involved in research on the topic of memory and brain function. We have the possibility of memory manipulation to contend with. The Defense Advanced Research Projects Agency (DARPA; https://www.darpa.mil) is a highly funded agency of the USA aimed at developing projects concerned with national security. When the defence department becomes involved, we can recognise how significant this aspect of brain function is to the human condition in terms of its potential. This raises ethical questions for some and provides fodder for conspiracy theories for others.

This subject is starting me thinking about a world full of fear rather than full of love, the latter of which I would prefer to concentrate on, so enough said about fear and control.

The question of whether your brain is separate from your mind is a debate that has continued for centuries. I am not about to enter that particular complex argument. I do, however, have one technique of how to locate yourself in the world.

I ask you the question, where are you? Are you in your foot? No, your foot is part of you, but certainly not where you are consciously. Are you in your face? Well, a bit closer but not quite there yet. Nor are you in the back of your head, even though you are focusing within the brain region. Most people I ask identify their exact location as being directly behind the eyes. That would anatomically place the centre of your being in the location of the amygdala.

Increasingly, doors are opening in multiple professional disciplines where academics and researchers are brave enough to explore the world of the invisible. But not all research is applauded by the establishment.

An English author and researcher in the field of parapsychology, Rupert Sheldrake, proposed the concept that "memory is inherent in nature" and that "natural systems … inherit a collective memory from all previous things of their kind" (Sheldrake, 2011, p. 1). Sheldrake proposed that "morphic resonance", as he calls it, means there is a telepathy-type interconnection between organisms. The hypothesis of morphic resonance also leads to a radically new interpretation of memory storage in the brain. Biologically, an individual inherits a collective memory from past members of the species, contributes to the collective memory and, in turn, affects other members of the species into the future (Sheldrake, 2011).

However, morphic resonance is not accepted by the wider scientific community, and Sheldrake's proposals relating to it have been largely criticised.

In the following quote, researcher and educator Zainab Amadahy (2018) explains more about memory, suggesting it may still linger somewhere in the atmosphere after death:

> From biofield theory, we can further speculate that, if our physical bodies are, at their core, nothing more than a collection of energy fields interacting with each other, death does not destroy the information contained in those fields. (para. 20)

If it is true that death does not destroy information attained by an individual, then ancestral knowledge and wisdom is floating around the cosmos ready to be accessed through the memory and communicated. The human brain has often been compared to a computer. Perhaps it needs rebooting now and then so that the random-access-memory storage system can be reactivated.

My analogy with this topic is through comparison of a human being with a television. A television relays information in the form of entertainment and knowledge to the viewer. It might be said that it is unconscious with no comprehension of where the information is coming from. The human mind can have a similar experience. Information is downloaded electrically from somewhere in the cosmos. Depending on the quality of the transmission, that information may be received successfully and then communicated on to other people.

I have been setting the framework in order to communicate my view that information sharing via memory-transfer-based time travel using something like electromagnetic fields is possible. This does not involve digital technology, nor is it dependent on linear time as we understand it. Information may travel across time and space upon a sophisticated network of electrically charged, connected atoms. I believe this system is already in place, being far more advanced than anything that can be duplicated artificially. But why bother duplicating? It already exists.

I propose we are biologically designed to share information. We are all living within a system that facilitates the process perfectly. In the same way that we are intrinsically and chemically designed to help one another, we are functioning within a world that allows us to communicate information across time and space using these electrical, interconnected energy fields. It is not only scientifically possible but also not that new. In fact, it is as old as time itself. Mental telepathy and clairvoyance are just some of the terms used to describe remote communicating using extrasensory processes. BCI may be seen as a technological version of biological memory transfer, in the same way mobile phones are a type of mental telepathy. Communicating with ancestors while in a trance state is a technique already known and still used by numerous indigenous cultures. The ability to receive information or communicate on another level using certain practices such as hallucinogenic plants is well documented. Time travel, without the need to physically relocate, has been around for a while.

Science, Metaphysics or Philosophy: Which Way?

This exploration of the internal landscape of the mind continues in the following paragraphs, where I document briefly other relevant information I have examined that relates to my experience.

Carl Jung, the Austrian neurologist and founder of psychoanalysis, seems a good place to start. I became interested in his term *collective unconscious*. In "The Significance of Constitution and Heredity in Psychology" (originally published in 1929), Jung wrote:

> And the essential thing, psychologically, is that in dreams, fantasies, and other exceptional states of mind the most far-fetched mythological motifs and symbols can appear autochthonously at any time, often, apparently, as the result of particular influences, traditions, and excitations working on the individual, but more often without any sign of them. These "primordial images," or "archetypes," as I have called them, belong to the basic stock of

the unconscious psyche and cannot be explained as personal acquisitions. Together they make up that psychic stratum which I have called the collective unconscious. (Jung, 1929/1969, p. 111)

"Exceptional states of mind" is what I believe I have lived through, and "acquisitions" from "the basic stock of the unconscious psyche" is the other experience I think I have had access to. With regard to the brain, in his book *The Mind's Past*, Michael Gazzaniga (2000) states:

> The baby does not learn trigonometry, but knows it; does not learn how to distinguish figure from ground, but knows it; does not need to learn, but knows, that when one object with mass hits another, it will move the object. … The vast human cerebral cortex is chock full of specialized systems ready, willing and able to be used for specific tasks. Moreover, the brain is built under tight genetic control. … As soon as the brain is built, it starts to express what it knows, what it comes with from the factory. And the brain comes loaded. (Gazzaniga, 2000, as cited by Treffert, 2015, para. 10)

In his book *What Counts: How Every Brain Is Hardwired for Math*, cognitive psychologist Brian Butterworth argues that we are born with brain circuits specialised for answering the question "How many?":

> The concept of numbers and the ability to recognize and process them is innate, part of everyone's intellectual apparatus whether they've had formal education or not. This "number instinct" is not dependent on basic intelligence or general knowledge, a fact which has implications for neuroscience and poses the question: why did man evolve with such specialized neural apparatus. It has been [said] that the social development of humans has been crucially affected by language, yet numbers have also been critical in the advancement of human culture. (Butterworth, 2000, para. 1)

According to Theosophy Wiki:

> The Akashic Records … are sometimes described as the "memory of nature". … [where] the cosmos has the ability to receive

and record "impressions" of everything that happens on the terrestrial plane. These records ... can be seen [and accessed] by some clairvoyants. ("Akashic Records," 2014, para. 1)

The akashic records were first mentioned in 1881, in Col. Olcott's book *The Buddhist Catechism*. There, he talks about "a permanency of records in the Akasha, and the potential capacity of man to read the same when he has evolved to the stage of true individual enlightenment." ("Akashic Records," 2014, General Description section)

Helena Petrovna Blavatsky, a Russian occultist, philosopher and author, co-founded the Theosophical Society in 1875. She was the leading theoretician of the esoteric religion of Theosophy. In her 1918 book, *The Theosophical Glossary*, she refers to the astral plane, as quoted on Theosophy Wiki:

When a person develops clairvoyance the plane that opens up to his or her perception is the one that is immediately "above" the physical—the astral plane (also called astral light). H. P. Blavatsky explained that on this plane we can find a record of everything that happened in the past: "According to Occult teaching the Astral light is ... the recorder of every thought; the universal mirror which reflects every event and thought as every being and thing, animate or inanimate. We call it the great Sea of Illusion, Maya." ("Akashic Records," 2014, Astral Plane section)

Perhaps there was an answer somewhere in philosophy. "The Allegory of the Cave" is a story from Book VII in Greek philosopher Plato's masterpiece *The Republic*, written in 517 BCE. The allegory uses the metaphor of a cave to examine the human condition and that of reality in a dialogue between Socrates and his disciple Glaucon:

Socrates tells Glaucon to imagine people living in a great underground cave, which is only open to the outside at the end of a steep and difficult ascent. Most of the people in the cave are prisoners chained facing the back wall of the cave so that they can neither move nor turn their heads. A great fire burns behind them, and all the prisoners can see are the shadows playing on the wall in front of them. They have been chained in that position all their lives.

There are others in the cave, carrying objects, but all the prisoners can see of them is their shadows. Some of the others speak, but there are echoes in the cave that make it difficult for the prisoners to understand which person is saying what. (Gill, 2019, paras. 2–3)

Socrates goes on to describe the difficulties a prisoner might have adapting after being freed from the chains (of reality):

When he sees that there are solid objects in the cave, not just shadows, he is confused. Instructors can tell him that what he saw before was an illusion, but at first, he'll assume his shadow life was the reality.

Eventually, he will be dragged out into the sun, be painfully dazzled by the brightness, and stunned by the beauty of the moon and the stars. Once he becomes accustomed to the light, he will pity the people in the cave and want to stay above and apart from them, but think of them and his own past no longer. The new arrivals will choose to remain in the light, but, says Socrates, they must not. Because for true enlightenment, to understand and apply what is goodness and justice, they must descend back into the darkness, join the men chained to the wall, and share that knowledge with them.

…

In the next chapter …, Socrates explains what he meant, that the cave represents the world, the region of life which is revealed to us only through the sense of sight. The ascent out of the cave is the journey of the soul into the region of the intelligible.

The path to enlightenment is painful and arduous, says Plato, and requires that we make four stages in our development:

1. Imprisonment in the cave (the imaginary world)

2. Release from chains (the real, sensual world)

3. Ascent out of the cave (the world of ideas)

4. The way back to help our fellows.

(Gill, 2019, paras. 4–7)

I sometimes feel I have personally been in that cave.

The following is an extract from *The Celestine Prophecy*, a 1993 adventure novel by James Redfield:

> "The Manuscript predicts," she went on, "that once we reach this critical mass, the entire culture will begin to take these coincidental experiences seriously. We will wonder, in mass, what mysterious process underlies human life on this planet. And it will be this question, asked at the same time by enough people, that will allow the other insights to also come into consciousness—because according to the Manuscript, when a sufficient number of individuals seriously question what's going on in life, we will begin to find out." (p. 9)

Skyharp

In 2015, I wrote a research report going to extreme lengths to highlight what I thought was world-changing research on time. I built an artwork, aka, a time machine—a machine for telling (astronomical) time.

This was well before I went to Mexico. I did my own, independent, prolonged and sustained study of the time cycles of the planets and how they relate to geometry. It was this that possibly set off an extrasensory perception somewhere in my mind. Or, more accurately, it activated some part of my memory—brain hardwiring that was compatible with the Maya worldview.

In a remote part of Australia, this art installation, *Skyharp* (Images 64 and 65), aligned with the equinox and solstice. It also incorporated the golden ratio. Twice a year, the shadow of the circles aligned perfectly, only for about 15 minutes, during the equinox. At all other times throughout the year, the pattern was discordant. Within the geometric boundaries of two interlocked circles, I uncovered the elementary mathematical processes from which to calculate the orbits of the visible planets and the moon. *Skyharp* encompassed eclipse cycles as well. The artwork used days as a measurement, similar to what the Maya did on their temple.

During this process, I began to realise how it may be possible to use time as a physical measurement within architecture. Some years later, to my surprise, I discovered it had already been done. Using the concept of time as measurement was integrated in a design over 1600 years earlier on a Maya temple in Mexico. Was it this artistic process that reprogrammed my mind and triggered an ability to decipher the Maya calendar and its relationship to architecture?

Perhaps the process of creating the artwork was part of some kind of initiation. Quite possibly, I had gained access to the great collective memory storage system I now believe is built metaphysically into the atmosphere surrounding the earth.

Image 64: **Skyharp** *art sculpture showing irregular shadow patterns on the background*

Image 65: **Skyharp** *art sculpture showing aligned circles during equinox*

Chapter 9

Is this the Warning of the Art of Aquarius?

The unexamined life is not worth living
—Socrates

A Collaboration Between Civilisations

I am almost certain somebody made it across the Atlantic Ocean, met with the Maya and integrated their cultural values with those of the locals. Of all the possibilities, it's the Phoenicians who stand out as the most likely candidates.

The obvious evidence is their unrivalled capacity as ocean-going mariners. This has been proven by the *Phoenicia* replica sailing ship with its successful trans-Atlantic crossing in 2019. But more than that, substantial social and philosophical evidence supports this theory.

The Phoenicians were not violent invaders. They were commercial traders. They had established trade routes throughout the Mediterranean, not by force, but by a philosophy of developing ongoing good relationships. Author and business negotiator Dr Habib Chamoun-Nicolas has studied the history of the Phoenicians, having published a book entitled *Negotiate Like a Phoenician: Discover TraDEAbLes* (2007). He believes the ancient Phoenicians always had a win-win philosophy whereby each member of a negotiation mutually benefited.

This approach contrasts markedly to what happened with the Spanish conquest. It may be true to say that the Phoenicians, who would have arrived much earlier, would have been received favourably by the people of Central America. The following observations were recorded by Columbus upon his first arrival in the Caribbean in 1492:

> They are very well formed, with handsome bodies and good faces. ... They do not carry arms nor are they acquainted with them. ... They should be good and intelligent servants. ... And these people are very gentle, and because of their desire to have some of our things and believing that nothing will be given to them without their giving something, and not having anything, they take what they can and then throw themselves into the water to swim. (Columbus, 1492, paras. 4–6)

Further testament to the strong possibility of cultural diffusion between the Phoenicians and the Maya is that geometry and the cubit are fundamental aspects of the design of the Temple of Kukulkan. These mathematical concepts of design and measurement create a common link with the Phoenicians. The six-pointed star can be traced as far back as the biblical era. It was the Phoenicians who built Solomon's Temple. The Seal of Solomon is a six-pointed star from the same era. It is clear that geometry was high on the list of priorities in design, as evidenced by the importance of using a particular unit of measure, the cubit, as documented in the Bible. Measurement and geometry are intrinsically linked, especially with regard to architecture. Pythagoras, the son of a Phoenician, is a high-profile mathematician and philosopher from the era. His contribution to geometry and mathematics is substantial proof of the significant role these disciplines played in this ancient society.

The foundation design principles of the Phoenicians' worldview are in harmony with those who designed and built the Temple of Kukulkan. Together with the Phoenicians' social values, which may have been similar to those of the early people of Mesoamerica, this suggests that intellectual concepts would have been shared had they met. Some lost chapters in world history may be exposed here if we are open to the possibility.

The accumulation of these peripheral links supports my contention that the Phoenicians would have collaborated successfully with the Maya.

Chapter 9 : Is this the Warning or the Art of Aquarius

By way of their remarkable negotiation skills, I propose they managed to influence the Maya designers to base the six-pointed star within the design of the Temple of Kukulkan and also to use a specific unit of measure. These design features were blended with the local recognition of the qualities of the Maya calendar.

The most probable timeframe when this occurred would be during or shortly after the Third Punic War (149–146 BCE). This conflict was between the Roman Republic and the Carthaginian Empire and resulted in the destruction of Carthage. Most likely, to escape enslavement and to re-establish their civilisation, a number of Phoenicians set sail for the New World. They knew the way already. However, this was the final one-way Ophir expedition.

Around 500 years later or thereabouts, the Temple of Kukulkan was built. Archaeologists suggest that around 400 CE was the timeframe for the beginning of the construction of Chichen Itza. It would have taken at least several decades to build a rapport with the local indigenous people. It may have taken additional decades for those involved to reach a consensus on the final layout design and more time again for construction.

Anthropological evidence supports possible trans-Atlantic contact between those of Middle Eastern origin and the Americas well before Columbus. Ancient-DNA specialist Eske Willerslev, of the University of Copenhagen in Denmark, found nearly one third of Native American genes come from west Eurasian people linked to the Middle East and Europe (Handwerk, 2013). This research challenges the theory that the Americas were initially populated entirely from East Asians as previously thought. These are the results from analysis of a newly sequenced genome. It is not clear to me whether the study included the Maya people.

This background of supporting evidence leads me to propose something that may be controversial, to say the least. That is, just as the Phoenicians built the first temple in Jerusalem, they may have also been instrumental in building what could be described as the third (Jewish) temple in Mexico. This might save somebody a lot of money by not bothering to go to the effort of building another one in Israel. It has already been done. You can thank me later.

It is conceivable both the 20-day and 13-day cycles fundamental to the 260-day Maya calendar could also be found within the dimensions of the upper temple. Resources were not available at the time of writing this book, so I am leaving that for another day, or for someone else with a passion and curiosity to investigate this observation further. More extensive research of the measurements of other surrounding structures at Chichen Itza may prove that 262 mm was a unit of measurement used throughout the design layout of the entire complex. I suspect this will be the case. There are a few similar measures to those used in the Temple of Kukulkan. Although I cannot verify it accurately at present, it appears the width of the ball court at Chichen Itza is approximately 116 days, identical to the height of Kukulkan.

Scholars who write articles about the Maya calendar invariably suggest its origin and usefulness is mainly linked to crop planting and harvesting, especially in reference to the 260-day calendar because its duration has no known astronomy cycle, as already stated. The same can be said for the 819-day calendar. It is foreseeable that the early tribes would have needed to rely on some cyclic reference to nature in order to maintain an agricultural subsistence. This assessment is predictable and not without credibility, yet it diminishes the intellectual capacity of the ancient Maya.

The capacity to analyse geometry using trigonometry, pi ratios and other mathematical calculations demonstrates an advanced intellectual capability on the part of the builders of the Temple of Kukulkan, whoever they may be. Moreover, to apply that same system to architecture using ratio and proportion, as demonstrated in this research, requires an advanced capacity to future-proof their intellectual knowledge. All this, using a single unit of measurement. The temple design required detailed analysis, intelligent planning and implementation, a knowledge of astronomy and artistic vision. These are the hallmarks of an extremely sophisticated society.

Closer examination of the stairway area shows every part of the temple was interrelated. What appears at first glance to be practical and purely decorative indicates each small measurement is a significant part of the whole design (Diagram 32).

Chapter 9 : Is this the Warning or the Art of Aquarius

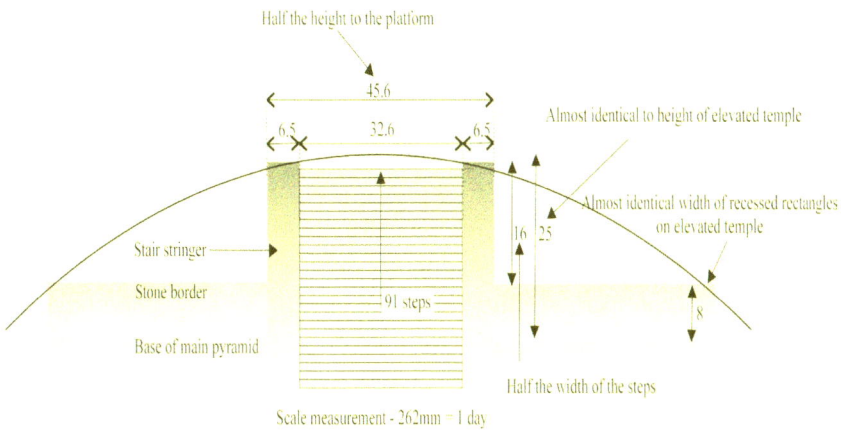

Diagram 32: Detail of stairway showing relationship of smaller measurements to the whole

The overwhelming evidence described here in this book demonstrates how time durations are integrated within a geometric model. Therefore, a complete reassessment of the origin of the calendar might be necessary. In my opinion, that reassessment should have geometry as the model from which to understand the calendar's complexity. I can state, almost without reservation, that the Maya calendar has its origins primarily in mathematics and geometry and, through that, we can understand its links to astronomy.

What Was Once Concealed Will Be Revealed

I am already pushing the boundaries with this investigation, so why not go all the way?

Let us suppose an invisible auric field surrounds the Temple of Kukulkan similarly as is suggested with human physiology. The designers wanted to recognise this as a mathematical reality. It is only perceivable by understanding the temple's dimensions. This may be stretching the imagination, yet this kind of thinking is not outside the capacity of the mystical Maya. Incorporating an aura would rectify the inconsistencies between the temple dimensions and the calendar.

What, then, would the dimensions of the aura be?

I suggest this invisible field has a width of 262 mm or one day. We know each day is important to the Maya, but how is one day important in science? It relates to the orbit of the earth and the one-day difference between 365.242 days and 366.242 days caused by the precession of the equinoxes.

A synodic year is the time it takes for a given planet to have a recurring alignment with the sun. For the sun, it is the time it takes to come to the same place on the ecliptic and is called a tropical year. A sidereal year, on the other hand, is the time taken for the sun to return to the same position with respect to the stars. A tropical year of 365.242 days has 366.242 sidereal days. There is a variation of one day. (University of Nebraska-Lincoln, n.d.)

A curious synchronicity exists between the mathematical variation of one day with regard to the axis rotation of the earth and the size relationship between the earth and the moon. That ratio is 1:3.66242 or almost exactly 3:11. I sometimes use this ratio in my art. I simply move the decimal point where it becomes possible to see a relationship; 366.242 becomes 3.66242. This number, 3.66242, matches the size ratio of the earth to the moon.

Equatorial diameter of earth = 12,756.2 km

Polar diameter of earth = **12,713.6** km

Equatorial diameter of moon = 3,476.2 km

Polar diameter of moon = **3,472** km

The above figures are reproduced from a NASA Space Science Data Coordinated Archive fact sheet (Williams, 2020). Dividing the polar diameter of the earth by 3.66242 equals the polar diameter of the moon to within about 0.7 kilometres accuracy:

$$12{,}713.6 \div 3.66242 = 3471.3 \text{ km}$$

This same calculation can be applied to the dimensions of the Temple of Kukulkan to find some comparatively interesting results.

Chapter 9 : Is this the Warning or the Art of Aquarius

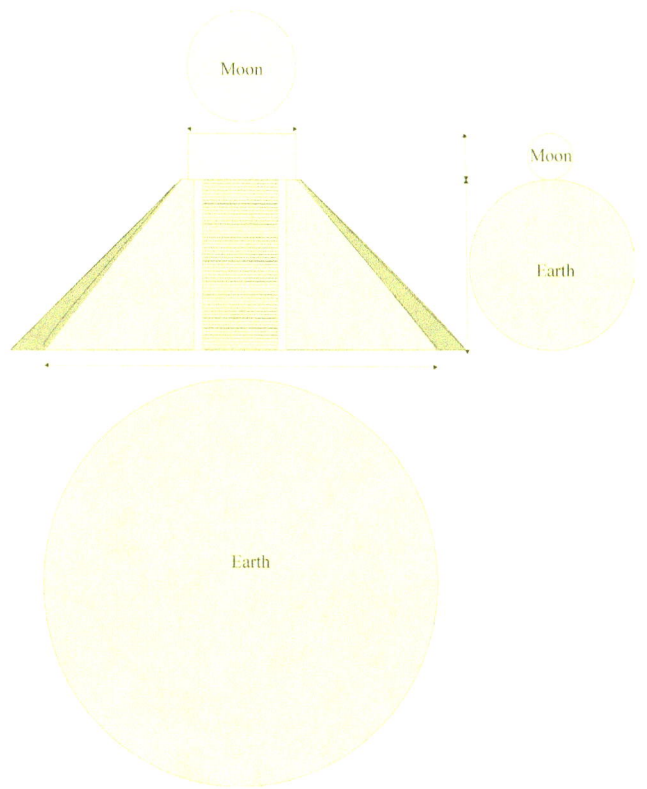

Diagram 33: The Temple of Kukulkan's design accurately reflects the proportional size ratio of the earth to the moon

The height to the temple platform in days, 91 (see Table 1, measurement G), divided by 3.66242 equals 24.8 days, which is the height of the elevated temple (see Table 1, measurement M1):

$$91 \div 3.66242 = 24.8 \text{ days}$$

Just in case we missed something, there is another example. The (mean) side lengths of the temple pyramid base, 211.5 days (see Table 1, measurement E), divided by 3.66242 equals 57.7 days:

$$211.5 \div 3.66242 = 57.7 \text{ days}$$

This is almost identical to the width of the elevated temple (see Table 1, measurement M2).

The Temple of Kukulkan accurately reflects the ratio of the earth to the moon. An accident, obviously. A coincidence, just like the use of an identical unit of measurement from a different civilisation across the Atlantic Ocean? I don't think so. The question should be asked, did the designers know the diameter relationship between the earth and the moon and apply that same knowledge to the temple architecture?

Diagram 34: **Skyharp** *sculpture showing earth-to-moon size ratio*

In my sculptural art project, *Skyharp* (Diagram 34), completed in 2015, I used this ratio because I understand it to have special aesthetic appeal in design. The art is arranged to link the cycles of astronomy mathematically with the equinox. This project was built to illustrate what I believe to be important—that is, we should endeavour to be constantly aware of the beauty and synchronicity of the cosmos, of which we are all a part. If our mind is occupied with such concepts, there is not a lot of time left for negative thought patterns.

This same ratio appears on the cover of this book (Diagram 35).

Chapter 9 : Is this the Warning or the Art of Aquarius

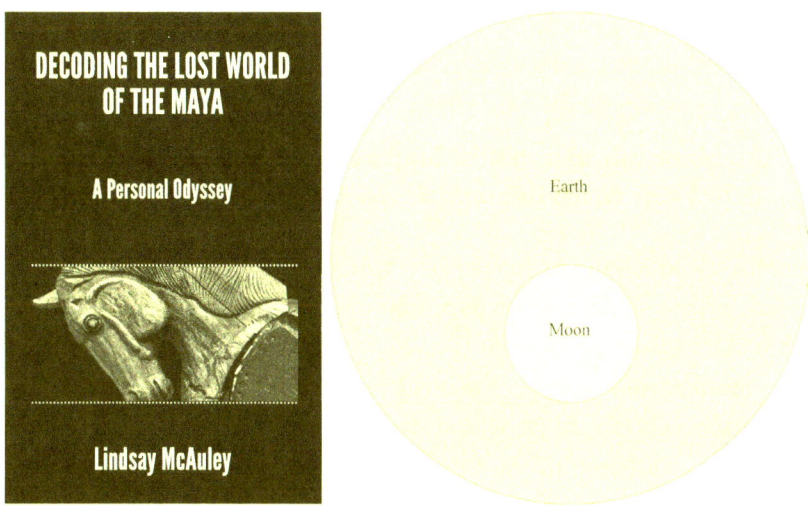

Diagram 35: Cover design showing earth-to-moon ratio

The mathematical research documented in this book suggests there should be a reappraisal not only of the Maya calendar but also of human origins and, therefore, the history of the world. Disregarding the possibility of alien intervention, we may have to consider, as confronting as it might be, that an advanced civilisation existed before the hunter-gatherer era. Perhaps a civilisation walked the earth that makes us look like lost children grappling in the dark when it comes to esoteric wisdom and scientific knowledge. We have just forgotten about this ancient lost tribe, who they were and where they came from.

So another Pandora's box is now open, not only concerning the possible geometric origin of the Maya calendar but also forcing us to consider who devised it. I believe no particular civilisation or individual from the last 10,000-year epoch, that is, pre-Anthropocene, can take credit for devising the calendar. I believe it is much older. What I am suggesting is that before the hunter-gatherer era, from a long-forgotten history, remnants of the mathematics somehow survived through the ages in fragments. Then, it was remembered by the Olmec and other civilisations such as the Maya and the Aztec. It was remembered, not created. It is being remembered by people of this current civilisation now. Gradually, little by little, it is being increasingly remembered over time as we uncover more of the source of its complexity. It is being downloaded to our conscious mind gradually from a giant internet-like server surrounding the earth, built metaphysically into the atmosphere.

The Maya calendar existed long before anyone from the last 10,000-year epoch can take the credit for devising it.

Something old fell out of the sky on 15 August 2019, as I was writing this book. It was as ancient as the mountains of Honduras, as old as the stone within the walls of Kukulkan. It tied everything together for me. I saw it as the masterstroke, and yet I somehow knew I could not take the credit for its discovery. It just arrived out of the blue. It linked the past with the present, the present with the future. It came like a thunderbolt shaking its way across the bow of the *Phoenicia*, thereby completing this investigation perfectly. The Merkabah had landed.

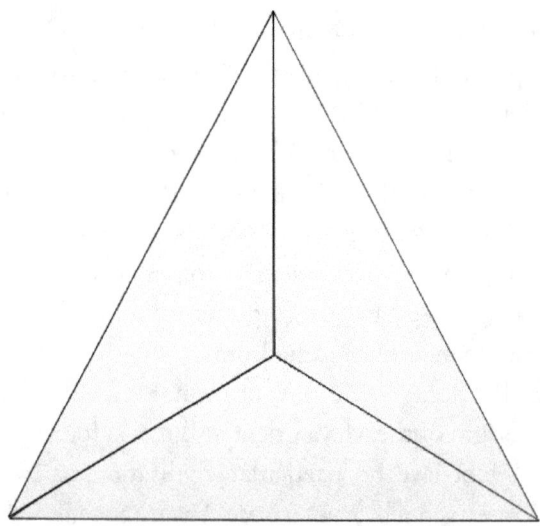

Diagram 36: A 3-dimensional tetrahedron

The meaning of the noun *Merkabah* is "thing to ride in, cart, or chariot" (Alziel, 2016, para. 1). The word is found in the Masoretic Text of the Hebrew Bible. The Merkabah is made up of two tetrahedrons interlocked to form a 3-dimensional shape. In two dimensions, it is a six-pointed star.

Chapter 9 : Is this the Warning or the Art of Aquarius

Diagram 37: Two tetrahedrons combined comprise what is known as a Merkabah

A Merkabah is a variation on the Star of David and the Seal of Solomon. Individually, it comprises two tetrahedrons (or triangular pyramids), each of which contains **four faces, four vertices** and six edges. Each face is triangular. The geometry relates perfectly to the extract from the ancient Maya text, the *Popol Vuh*, where the following poetic description can be found:

> **the fourfold siding, fourfold cornering,
> measuring, fourfold staking,**
> halving the cord, stretching the cord
> in the sky, on the earth,
> **the four sides, the four corners**, as it is said,
> by the Maker, Modeler, ...
> (D. Tedlock, 1996, pp. 63–64, emphasis added)

I see this extract as a poetic description of the geometry of a tetrahedron upon which the Merkabah is founded. The *Popol Vuh* is a foundation narrative of the Maya creation myth. Originally it was communicated orally, so its actual age is unknown. It is relayed via the memory. The text features the exploits of two central characters, the Hero Twins, Hunahpú and Xbalanqué (Annenburg Foundation, 2010; D. Tedlock, 1996). The narrative creates links between this ancient text and the geometry of the four-sided tetrahedron that are as clear to me as crystal. It ties all the elements of this investigation together:

- The Merkabah with the ratio and proportion of Kukulkan.
- The Temple of Kukulkan with the Maya calendar.
- The measurement standard used in construction.

The cubit and span measurements I used to analyse the dimensions of the temple are the same as those used in ancient biblical texts of Ezekiel of the same era. In Jewish Kabbalah mysticism, the Merkabah is sometimes referenced to Ezekiel's vision of the "four living beings" and the chariot upon which they ride (Alziel, 2016).

... four faces, four vertices ...
... the fourfold siding, fourfold cornering, measuring, fourfold staking ... the four sides, the four corners ...

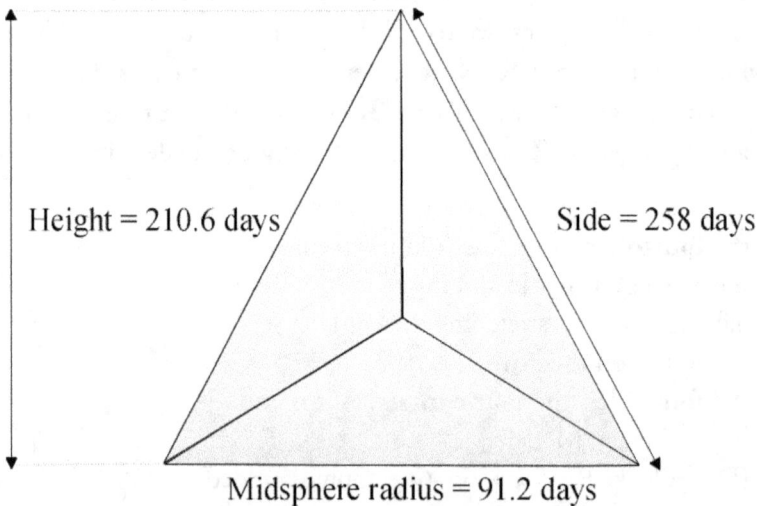

Diagram 38: A 3-dimensional tetrahedron showing four corners and four sides

It is conceivable that a tetrahedron (i.e. the Merkabah) was the basis of the architectural design using a 262-mm unit of measurement scale. This is reaffirmed in the following calculations analysing the dimensions of a proposed tetrahedron used in the design (Diagram 38) and comparing them with the measurements of the Temple of Kukulkan at Chichen Itza:

Chapter 9 : Is this the Warning or the Art of Aquarius

- Edge length = 258 days, identical to overall temple width (distance between stringers)
- Height = 210.6 days, almost identical to the mean side length of the pyramid base, 211.5 days
- Midsphere radius = 91.2 days, equal to the number of steps to reach the temple (-0.2).

$$a = 258$$
$$h = \frac{a}{3} \times \sqrt{6}$$
$$r_m = \frac{a}{4} \times \sqrt{2}$$

In writing this book, I feel the background of how this information came about is as important as the content. My passage through this maze is equally significant should someone else have had this kind of experience or be currently in the process. This pathway is not easy. It can be painfully tedious and annoying. It is also challenging, rewarding and, most of all, personally insightful. It has been my struggle.

It strikes me as remarkable that mathematics was the key to finding a resolution to this traditionally archaeological field of investigation. The decoding of the Temple of Kukulkan essentially relied on locating the scale measurement used in construction. The key to the maths was in the height of the steps. Without this observation, there would be no knowledge of how the designers created a stationary calendar frozen within its architecture. There would be no understanding of the creative intelligence required to encode the mathematics within ratio and proportion. By using archaeology qualifications alone, this would be virtually impossible. It required another set of skills entirely. This included a limited knowledge of mathematics and astronomy, a proficiency for abstract analysis and some artistic perception. A bit of time-travel experience came in handy, along with a teaspoon of clairvoyance. I have acquired some of these skills during my life; others are part of my nature. Non-academic research and opinions do have some value.

But essentially, more than anything, this work came as a result of remembering.

The world is not the same place for a lot of people. Something is afoot. That is no big secret. Many people claim to have had a transformative experience. Personally, I believe I have made contact with a philosophy lost to our modern world and, through the journey, now have an understanding of the motivations driving the builders of the Temple of Kukulkan, whoever they were. I have reconnected in some way. I have remembered. I have climbed the steps toward the metaphysical temple of the ancient Maya, who have built the physical world in the image of the cosmos, who have strived to bring heaven to earth, to harmonise the celestial with the terrestrial.

Image 66: Tourists viewing the Temple of Kukulkan

Twice a year, during the equinox, the illusion of the body of a serpent descends the stairway. Perhaps, as the legend goes, Kukulkan, the feathered serpent, is bringing ancient wisdom down from the temple. People gather from around the world in increasing numbers to witness this interplay of light and shadow. Are they subconsciously drawn to this place, as though waiting for something? On some level, are they able to perceive the geometric aura that surrounds the building?

Chapter 9 : Is this the Warning or the Art of Aquarius

Diagram 39: Proposed 3-dimensional tetrahedron superimposed on the Temple of Kukulkan

Perhaps a great star is hovering over the temple waiting to take the people to the next level of clarity. As consciousness is raised step by step, day by day upwards to the elevated temple, the metaphorical chariot is there waiting to carry the spirit beyond into the realms of parallel universes. Hang on! It will be the ride of a lifetime.

Now, when I look at the Temple of Kukulkan, I see more than a pleasing shape of symmetrically assembled rocks. Just as the human body is said to have an aura, I see the mathematics and geometry invisible to the naked eye. Somehow I have tuned in to communicate some of what needed to be remembered. I became one with the Maya worldview, if only for a brief time. I am thankful for this experience, for being led, somewhat reluctantly, into an altered state of mind.

After all of this—my inner questions together with the challenges of presenting the geometry and mathematical calculations—after all the conflict and difficulty it took to bring this book together, what I do know for certain, without question: I have travelled a remarkable mystical journey of the mind, body and spirit.

In the Preface of this book, I suggested I had been part of a miraculous process. I mentioned that to a friend and she replied, "Aren't we all?"

Well yes, we are. We are all part of this miracle called life.

Epilogue: Now

The history of the world has changed. In 2020, it has changed so dramatically, our way of life may never be the same.

"The world cannot go on like this." That comment, I have heard numerous times lately. I should add that what I mean by "lately" is well before the coronavirus pandemic, otherwise known as COVID-19, was ever heard of. As I write this, it swarms out over the planet, putting every nation on earth on a war-like footing. Like a microscopic grim reaper, it stalks its way into busy subways, crowded churches, quiet country lanes and the family home. This predator seeks out places where humans dwell. There is little rest for anything comprised of flesh and blood. The world cannot go on like this and now, with this disease to contend with, well, it isn't, is it?

It is relevant and timely that I should comment on this phenomenon within the context of my research concerning the Maya.

We cannot keep poisoning the atmosphere. We cannot keep living in conflict with one another in this rat race, running to and fro, racing up and down the highway like lemmings over a cliff. The world cannot go on living in fear while treating wildlife as disposable items. Something had to fracture. And it has.

Many of us were anticipating a major event of some kind was going to happen sooner or later. Many people might be saying, "I didn't see this particular circumstance coming, but I knew an agent of change in some form was on its way". Now, we are forced into social isolation to contemplate this sudden, dramatic reshaping of global society.

Almost every person on earth, 7.7 billion of us, is suddenly being tossed about, confused and disorientated, waiting for the storm to calm.

Epilogue : Now

Everything seems to be fluid and changeable, unpredictable, as though there is nothing solid to hold on to. Many of us want to find a way back to the place where we were before. Familiarity with an uncertain future is better than unfamiliarity with an uncertain future.

Having built a complex civilisation such as ours, chewing at earth's resources like a hungry lion, we may be forced into a readjustment of values more quickly than anticipated. As we watch from behind our curtains the events unfolding and changing rapidly before our eyes, we would do well to remember the experience of the Maya.

Their civilisation stopped abruptly. Ours may be facing the same sudden decline with a potential fall from the material mountain we have built so voraciously. Of course, I have heard the saying that there is supposed to be a silver lining in every calamity. So where are the benefits in this global NDE (near-death experience)? For many thousands, it has become very real. When we come out the other side of this challenge, if we survive this intact and it proves to be temporary, it is possibly the best wake-up call ever. We are at a moment of imposed introspection, a chance to examine our worldview and values.

It has been said before. There needs to be a change in attitude within leadership in the world right now. Not in a couple of years. Now. We need to realign humanity spiritually with the cosmos, with the seasons, with nature and with each other. As the shamans and mystics have argued over the millennia, we need to bring the celestial down to the terrestrial.

The gift to us all is this wonderous blue sphere spinning through space in perfect mathematical harmony. Embrace it. That might be the message for us all as we pivot on this four-way axis of fear and love, ignorance and wisdom. The Maya have already been through this. They have experienced it. It is built into their collective memory. The cultural architecture of humanity needs a realignment. In my opinion, who better to draw upon for guidance in this conflict of human affairs than the mystical Maya? They are not extinct. These people still breath the air of their ancestors. Within the blood of their veins, ancient wisdom still flows.

Against this background, I advocate, loud and clear, reinstating the Maya civilisation. Not as soon as possible. **Now.**

Glossary of Terms

Aztec	When used to describe ethnic groups, the term Aztec refers to several Nahuatl-speaking peoples of central Mexico in the Postclassic period of Mesoamerican chronology, especially the Mexica, the ethnic group that had a leading role in establishing the hegemonic empire based at Tenochtitlan.
b'ak'tun cycle	The b'ak'tun is a time cycle in the Maya Long Count calendar containing 144,000 days, which is equal to 394.26 tropical years.
Chac Mool	A Chac Mool (also spelled chacmool or chac-mool) is a form of pre-Columbian Mesoamerican sculpture depicting a reclining figure supporting itself on its elbows and holding a bowl or disk.
CyArk	"CyArk is a non-profit organization founded in 2003 to digitally record, archive and share the world's most significant cultural heritage" (CyArk, 2020, para. 1).
Francísco Ximénez	Francísco Ximénez (November 28, 1666 – c. 1729) was a Dominican priest who is known for his conservation of an indigenous Maya narrative known today as *Popol Vuh*.
golden ratio	The golden ratio is defined by mathematicians as a relation in which the smaller unit is to the larger unit as the larger is to the sum. a:b = b:(a+b). The name for this ratio is *phi*. Its numeric value is 1.618034.
Haab	The Haab is the Maya calendar cycle most similar to the Christian calendar. With 365 days in its count, it is obviously based on solar observations. It is sometimes called the "vague" year because, unlike the Christian calendar, it does not include a leap year.

Glossary of Terms

K'iche' people	K'iche' are indigenous peoples of the Americas and one of the Maya peoples. The K'iche' language is a Mesoamerican language in the Mayan language family.
k'in	The Maya year has a basic unit called a k'in, a word that means day, sun, etc. It is defined as the length of one day.
lidar	Lidar (also called LIDAR, LiDAR and LADAR) stands for light detection and ranging and "is a surveying method that measures distance to a target by illuminating the target with pulsed light and measuring the reflected pulses with a sensor" ("Lidar," 2020, para. 1).
Maya calendar	The Maya calendar was used in pre-Columbian Mesoamerica and is still used by many contemporary cultures in Central American countries such as Guatemala and Mexico.
Maya codices	Maya codices (singular codex) are folding books written by the pre-Columbian Maya civilisation in Maya hieroglyphic script on Mesoamerican bark paper.
Mesoamerica	Mesoamerica is a region and culture defined as the area in the Americas extending approximately from central Mexico to Belize, Guatemala, El Salvador, Honduras, Nicaragua and Costa Rica.
Popol Vuh	*Popol Vuh* (also *Popol Wuj*) is a cultural narrative that recounts the mythology and history of the K'iche' people who inhabit the Guatemalan Highlands northwest of present-day Guatemala City.
Quetzalcoatl	A Mesoamerican deity or supernatural being. The name means "feathered serpent".
Shaman	A person regarded as having access to, and influence in, the world of good and evil spirits, especially among some peoples of northern Asia and North America. Typically, such people enter a trance state during a ritual, and practise divination and healing.

Solomon's temple	The Hebrew Bible states that the temple was constructed under Solomon, king of the United Kingdom of Israel and Judah and, that during the Kingdom of Judah, the temple was dedicated to Yahweh. It is said to have housed the Ark of the Covenant. Jewish historian Josephus said that "the temple was burnt four hundred and seventy years, six months, and ten days after it was built" ("Solomon's Temple," 2020).
square root	A square root of a number is a value that, when multiplied by itself, gives the number.
Temple of Kukulkan	Known in Spanish as *El Castillo*, meaning "the castle", the Temple of Kukulkan is a Mesoamerican step pyramid that dominates the centre of the Chichen Itza archaeological site in the Mexican state of Yucatán.
Toltec	The Toltec culture is an archaeological Mesoamerican culture that dominated a state centred in Tula, Hidalgo, Mexico in the early Postclassic period of Mesoamerican chronology (ca. 900–1168 CE).
Tzolkin	The 260-day Tzolkin, or sacred calendar, is the oldest calendar cycle known in Mesoamerica, dating back to at least 600 BCE. While some scholars are still searching for an astronomical basis for this cycle, most agree it was based on the nine-month human gestation period. As a testimony to the Tzolkin's centrality to Maya culture, it is still observed today among traditional Maya groups.
Vitruvius	Marcus Vitruvius Pollio (ca. 80–70 BCE – after ca. 15 BCE), commonly known as Vitruvius, was a Roman author, architect, civil engineer and military engineer during the 1st century BCE, known for his multi-volume work entitled De architectura (Vitruvius, 1914). His discussion of perfect proportion in architecture and the human body led to the famous Renaissance drawing by Leonardo da Vinci of Vitruvian Man ("Vitruvius," 2020).

References

Akashic Records. (2014, August 5). In *Theosophy Wiki*. https://theosophy.wiki/en/Akashic_Records

Alziel. (2016, June 20). *The Merkabah*. 13 Dimensions. http://www.thirteen-dimensions.com/merkabah/

Amadahy, Z. (2018, June 19). Accessing embodied ancestral knowledge. *The Peak Magazine*. http://peakmag.net/reclamation/accessing-embodied-ancestral-knowledge/

Annenburg Foundation. (2010). *Invitation to world literature: Popol Vuh—Read the text*. Annenburg Learner. https://www.learner.org/series/invitation-to-world-literature/popol-vuh/popol-vuh-read-the-text/

Antonio de Montezinos. (2020, April 3). In *Wikipedia*. https://en.wikipedia.org/wiki/Antonio_de_Montezinos

Augustus Le Plongeon. (2020, April 18). In *Wikipedia*. https://en.wikipedia.org/wiki/Augustus_Le_Plongeon

Baktun. (2020, March 12). In *Wikipedia*. https://en.wikipedia.org/wiki/Baktun

Benford, G. (1999). *Deep time: How humanity communicates across millennia*. Bard.

Borschel-Dan, A. (2018, October 8). *Christopher Columbus: The hidden Jew?* The Times of Israel. https://www.timesofisrael.com/christopher-columbus-the-hidden-jew/

Bricker, H. M., & Bricker, V. R. (2011). *Astronomy in the Maya Codices*. American Philosophical Society.Chanier, T. (2015, January 12). *On the origin of the different Mayan calendars*. HAL Archives. https://hal.archives-ouvertes.fr/hal-01018037v2/document

Butterworth, B. (1999). *What counts: how every brain is hardwired for math*. Papermac. https://www.amazon.com.au/Mathematical-Brain-Brian-Butterworth/dp/0333766105

Campbell, J. (1949). *The hero with a thousand faces*. Pantheon Books.

Carson, B. (2008, January 11). Dr. Ben Carson. In *Religion & Ethics News-Weekly*. PBS. https://www.pbs.org/wnet/religionandethics/2008/01/11/january-11-2008-dr-ben-carson/656/

Cassidy, P. J., & Poznyakoff, S. (n.d.). *GNU Collaborative International Dictionary of English*. Retrieved May 7, 2020, from https://gcide.gnu.org.ua/

Central Intelligence Agency. (n.d.). *Guatemala*. https://www.cia.gov/library/readingroom/collection/guatemala

Chamoun-Nicolas,. H. (2007). *Negotiate like a Phoenician: Discover tradeables*. Keynegotiations.

Chanier, T. (2015, January 12). *On the origin of the different Mayan calendars*. HAL Archives. https://hal.archives-ouvertes.fr/hal-01018037v2/document

CNET. (2019, July 17). *Elon Musk's Neuralink presentation* [Video]. YouTube. https://youtu.be/lA77zsJ31nA

Cohn, D., Passel, J. S., & Gonzalez-Barrera, A. (2017, December 7). *Rise in U.S. immigrants from El Salvador, Guatemala and Honduras outpaces growth from elsewhere*. Pew Research Center. https://www.pewresearch.org/hispanic/2017/12/07/rise-in-u-s-immigrants-from-el-salvador-guatemala-and-honduras-outpaces-growth-from-elsewhere/

Columbus, C. (1492). *Journal*. https://www.swarthmore.edu/SocSci/bdorsey1/41docs/01-col.html.

Courtney, E. (n.d.). Microbes and your memory: The gut–brain connection. *Hyperbiotics*. https://www.hyperbiotics.com/blogs/recent-articles/113778182-probiotics-and-your-memory-the-gut-brain-connection

CyArk. (2020). *Our mission*. https://www.cyark.org/about/

Early English Books. (n.d.). *The hope of Israel*. http://name.umdl.umich.edu/A89453.0001.001

Galilei, G. (1957). *Discoveries and opinions of Galileo* (S. Drake, Ed. & Trans.). Doubleday. (Original work *Il Saggiatore* published 1623)

Gill, N. S. (2019, August 11). The allegory of the cave from *The Republic* of Plato. *ThoughtCo*. https://www.thoughtco.com/the-allegory-of-the-cave-120330

Handwerk, B. (2013, November 22). "Great Surprise"—Native Americans have west Eurasian origins. *National Geographic*. https://www.nationalgeographic.com/news/2013/11/131120-science-native-american-people-migration-siberia-genetics/

Hipparchus. (2020, April 12). In *Wikipedia*. https://en.wikipedia.org/wiki/Hipparchus

Holy Bible, New International Version. (2020). Bible Gateway. https://www.biblegateway.com/ (Original work published 1973)

House of Joseph (LDS Church). (2020, February 18). In *Wikipedia*. https://en.wikipedia.org/wiki/House_of_Joseph_(LDS_Church)

India Today. (2019, December 18). *What is NRC: All you need to know about National Register of Citizens.* https://www.indiatoday.in/india/story/what-is-nrc-all-you-need-to-know-about-national-register-of-citizens-1629195-2019-12-18

Instituto Nacional de Antropología e Historia. (2020, February 5). In *Wikipedia*. https://en.wikipedia.org/wiki/Instituto_Nacional_de_Antropolog%C3%ADa_e_Historia

Jenkins, J. M. (1995, February). *Venus, moon and the Tzolkin Calendar*. Alignment 2012. http://alignment2012.com/fap14.html

Jung, C. (1969). The significance of constitution and heredity in psychology. In G. Adler & R. Hull (Eds. & Trans.), *Collected works of C. G. Jung: Vol. 8. Structure & dynamics of the psyche* (2nd ed., pp. 107–113). Princeton University Press. https://www.jungiananalysts.org.uk/wp-content/uploads/2018/07/C. G.Jung-Collected-Works-Volume-8-The-Structure-and-Dynamics-of-the-Psyche.pdf (Original work published 1929)

Kasparis, C. (2011). *2012—The great shift*. AuthorHouse.

King James Bible. (2020). King James Bible Online. https://www.kingjamesbibleonline.org/ (Original work published 1769)

Kluger, J. (2012, May 14). Found: The oldest Maya calendar (and no, the world's still not ending). *Time*. http://content.time.com/time/health/article/0,8599,2114645,00.html

Kraus, H. P. (1970). *Sir Francis Drake: A pictorial biography*. https://www.loc.gov/rr/rarebook/catalog/drake/drake-6-caribraid.html

Krüger, C. (2014). *Rub out my history*. Strategic Book Publishing.

Lidar. (2020, March 19). In *Wikipedia.* https://en.wikipedia.org/w/index.php?title=Lidar&oldid=946396517

Maudslay, A. C., & Maudslay, A. P. (2011). *A glimpse at Guatemala, and some notes on the ancient monuments of Central America.* Cambridge Library Collection (Archaeology). https://doi.org/10.1017/CBO9780511686962 (Original work published 1899)

McLeod, A. (2016). *Astronomy in the ancient world: Early and modern views on celestial events.* Springer International.

McLuskey, S. C. (1998). *Astronomies and cultures in early medieval Europe.* Cambridge University Press.

Michael, J. (1983). *New view over Atlantis.* Thames and Hudson.

Milbrath, S. (1999). *Star gods of the Maya: Astronomy in art, folklore, and calendars.* University of Texas Press. https://www.academia.edu/2762803/Star_Gods_of_the_Maya_Astronomy_in_Art_Folklore_and_Calendars

O'Brien, P. J., & Christiansen, H. D. (1986). An ancient Maya measurement system. *American Antiquity, 51*(1), 136–151.

Oliver, M. (2019, February 7). 10 strange facts about Pythagoras: Mathematician and cult leader. *Listverse.* https://listverse.com/2017/04/26/10-strange-facts-about-pythagoras-mathematician-and-cult-leader/

Peck, D. T. (2005). *Yucatan: From prehistoric times to the great Maya revolt of 1546.* Xlibris Corporation.

Powell, C. (1997). *A new view on Maya astronomy* [Master's thesis, The University of Texas at Austin]. Maya Exploration Center. https://www.mayaexploration.org/pdf/A%20New%20View%20on%20Maya%20Astronomy.pdf

Powell, C. (2010). *The shapes of sacred space: A proposed system of geometry used to lay out and design Maya art and architecture and some implications concerning Maya cosmology* [Doctoral dissertation, The University of Texas at Austin]. Texas ScholarWorks. https://repositories.lib.utexas.edu/handle/2152/ETD-UT-2010-08-1700

Putnam, L. (2002). *The company they kept: Migrants and the politics of gender in Caribbean Costa Rica, 1870–1960.* The University of North Carolina Press.

Queensland Brain Institute. (2018, July 23). *Where are memories stored in the brain?* The University of Queensland. https://qbi.uq.edu.au/brain-basics/memory/where-are-memories-stored

Redfield, J. (1993). *The celestine prophecy*. Warner Books.

Rice, P. M. (2007). *Maya calendar origins: Monuments, mythistory, and the materialization of time*. University of Texas Press.

Rubik, B., Muehsam, D., Hammerschlag, R., & Jain, S. (2015). Biofield science and healing: History, terminology, and concepts. *Global Advances in Health and Medicine, 4*(Suppl), 8–14. https://doi.org/10.7453/gahmj.2015.038.suppl

Rubik, B., Pavek, R., Greene, E., Laurence, D., Ward, R., & Al, E. (1995). Manual healing methods. In B. Rubik et al. (Eds.), *Alternative medicine: Expanding medical horizons: A report to the National Institutes of Health on alternative medical systems and practices in the United States* (pp. 113–157). US Government Printing Office.

Saccoccio, D. (2017). *Spirit whirled: The deaf Pheonicians*. Dylan Saccoccio.

Salas, J. (2016, September 13). *Welcome to the Anthropocene: "We have now changed the Earth's cycle"*. El País. https://english.elpais.com/elpais/2016/09/12/inenglish/1473683883_859025.html

Sheldrake, R. (2011). *The presence of the past: Morphic resonance and the habits of nature* (revised edition). Icon Books.

Shih, J. J., Krusienski, D. J., & Wolpaw, J. R. (2012). Brain–computer interfaces in medicine. *Mayo Clinic Proceedings, 87*(3), 268–279. https://doi.org/10.1016/j.mayocp.2011.12.008

Solomon's Temple. (2020, May 7). In *Wikipedia*. https://en.wikipedia.org/wiki/Solomon%27s_Temple

Statista. (2019, December 5). *Number of visitors to Chichén Itzá archeological site in Mexico from 2009 to 2018*. https://www.statista.com/statistics/1078691/chichen-itza-mayan-archaeological-site-visitors/

Steffens, G. (2018, October 23). Changing climate forces desperate Guatemalans to migrate. *National Geographic*. https://www.nationalgeographic.com/environment/2018/10/drought-climate-change-force-guatemalans-migrate-to-us/

Stephens, J. L. (1843). *Incidents of travel in Central America, Chiapas and Yucatan*. Harper & Brothers.

Stewart, P. (2007). *The spiritual science of the stars: A guide to the architecture of the spirit*. Inner Traditions.

Tedlock, B. (1983). *Time and the Highland Maya*. University of New Mexico Press.

Tedlock, D. (Trans.). (1996). *Popol Vuh: The Mayan book of the dawn of life* (rev. ed.). Touchstone.

Ten Lost Tribes. (2020, May 7). In *Wikipedia*. https://en.wikipedia.org/wiki/Ten_Lost_Tribes

The Editors of Encyclopedia Britannica. (2020a, January 1). Diego De Landa. In *Encyclopedia Britannica*. https://www.britannica.com/biography/Diego-de-Landa

The Editors of Encyclopedia Britannica. (2020b, January 30). Star of David. In *Encyclopedia Britannica*. https://www.britannica.com/topic/Star-of-David

Treffert, D. (2015). Genetic memory: How we know things we never learned. *Scientific American*. https://blogs.scientificamerican.com/guest-blog/genetic-memory-how-we-know-things-we-never-learned/

UNESCO. (n.d.). *Pre-Hispanic city of Chichen-Itza*. UNESCO World Heritage List. https://whc.unesco.org/en/list/483

United Nations. (n.d.). Refugees. https://www.un.org/en/sections/issues-depth/refugees/

University of Nebraska-Lincoln. (n.d.). *Sidereal vs. synodic motions*. Astronomy Education at the University of Nebraska-Lincoln. https://astro.unl.edu/naap/motion3/sidereal_synodic.html

Vitruvius. (1914). *The ten books on architecture* (M. H. Morgan, Trans.). Lexundria. https://lexundria.com/vitr/1.2/mg (Original work published ca. 1st century B.C.E.)

Vitruvius. (2020). In *Wikipedia*. https://en.wikipedia.org/wiki/Vitruvius

Wiesenthal, S. (1973). *Sails of hope: The secret mission of Christopher Columbus*. MacMillan Publishing Company.

Williams, D. R. (2020, January 13). *Moon fact sheet*. NASA Space Science Data Coordinated Archive. https://nssdc.gsfc.nasa.gov/planetary/factsheet/moonfact.html

Wright, F. L. (n.d.). *Frank Lloyd Wright quotes*. All Great Quotes. https://www.allgreatquotes.com/quote-145147

Appendix

Table A1: 819-day Maya calendar temple reference and comparative values

Temple reference	Observed value	Process	Maya calendar reference (true value)	Variation to Maya calendar (days)	% error	Ref.	Chapter
Cir. of circle 819 days (Plan) Site ref. **A1**	819	Assigned value	819	0	0	Dia. 6,7,8,9,10,21	3
Cir. of circle 819 days (Elevation) Site ref. **A1**	819	Assigned value	819	0	0	Dia. 13	3

Table A2: 365-day Maya calendar temple reference and comparative values

Temple reference	Observed value	Process	Maya calendar reference (true value)	Variation to Maya calendar (days)	% error	Ref.	Chapter
Proposed diagonal length (Plan) Site ref. **D**	364.9	$258 \times \sqrt{2}$ = 364.9	365	0.1	0.03	Dia. 12,16, 21	3

Table A3: 260-day Maya calendar temple reference and comparative values

Temple reference	Observed value	Process	Maya calendar reference (true value)	Variation to Maya calendar (days)	% error	Ref.	Chapter
Diameter of circle Site ref. A2	260.7	$819 \div \pi$ $= 260.7$	260	0.7	0.27	Dia. 6,7,8, 9,10,21	3

Table A4: 210-day Maya calendar temple reference and comparative values

Temple reference	Observed value	Process	Maya calendar reference (true value)	Variation to Maya calendar (days)	% error	Ref.	Chapter
Length of side of pyramid base Site ref. E	210.9	$819 \div \pi \div 2 \times 1.618 = 210.9$	210	0.9	0.43	Dia. 17,21	3

Table A5: 117-day Maya calendar temple reference and comparative values

Temple reference	Observed value	Process	Maya calendar reference (true value)	Variation to Maya calendar (days)	% error	Ref.	Chapter
Overall height Site ref. F	116.6	$819 \div \pi \div \sqrt{5}$ $= 116.6$	117	0.4	0.34	Dia. 13,21	3
Length of side Site ref. I	117.2	hypotenuse $= 91^\wedge + 74^\wedge$ $= 117.2$	117	0.2	0.17	Dia. 12	3

Appendix

Table A6: Summary of Maya calendar comparative values and error margins

Maya calendar	True value	Observed value	% error
819-day	819	819	0
365-day (Haab)	365	364.9	0.03
260-day (Tzolkin)	260	260.7	0.27
210-day	210	210.9	0.43
117-day	117	116.0	0.34
		117.2	0.17
Venus sidereal duration	224.7	226	0.58
Mercury synodic period	115.88	116	0.10

Acknowledgements and Image Credits

With grateful assistance from:

Captain Philip Beale (https://www.phoeniciansbeforecolumbus.com)

Ralph Lante and Alex Rixon from Aerometrex Limited (CyArk 3-dimensional scan analysis) https://www.aerometrex.com.au

Julia Macdonald-Buchanan

Dr Mike Symonds: Maths tutoring

Charlotte Cottier: Editing

Kirsty Ogden: Book design and publishing mentoring

Rebecca McCallion: Proofreading

Cheeran Lo Cheuk Yan: Graphic art (maps)

Babette McAuley: Back cover photograph

Special thanks to:

Jan Richards

Lee McCloud

Artwork design, diagrams, maps and photographic images: Lindsay McAuley, with the exception of the following:

- Image 1: CyArk 3-dimensional lidar image of the Temple of Kukulkan: CyArk & Partners
- Image 6: Early photograph of the Temple of Kukulkan (taken by Teobert Maler 1892): Wikimedia Commons

- Image 8: The Dresden Codex, also known as the *Codex Dresdensis* (replica housed in Museo Regional de Antropología, Villahermosa, Mexico): Wikimedia Commons
- Image 9: Egyptian cubit rod in the Liverpool World Museum (photograph by Dave Lightbody): Released into the public domain by the author
- Image 15: Artistic representation of Solomon's Temple, 10th century BCE: Illumination by Jean Fouquet from a 15th century French edition of Flavius Josephus's *Antiquities of the Jews*
- Image 19: Egyptian royal cubit, Department of Egyptian Antiquities, Louvre Museum: Unknown author
- Image 22: The stele of the Code of Hammurabi (Babylon) depicts the king holding what may be interpreted as a measurement rod: Unknown author
- Image 53: Ceremony at Tikal, Guatemala: Jerson Gonzalez

Author's image reproductions authorised by: Instituto Nacional de Antropología e Historia (National Institute of Anthropology and History), Mexico.

About the Author

Lindsay McAuley grew up living close to nature on a sheep and cattle station in outback Queensland, Australia, where he first acquired an interest in astronomy, art and metaphysics.

A career in the art of film and photography helped Lindsay develop skills in writing. As an extension to his artistic nature, he obtained a certificate in art and went on to win awards as a visual artist.

Lindsay's artwork has featured in several group and solo art exhibitions, including a fine-art photography exhibition entitled *Skyharp*. This documented the changing light of the natural environment and its effect on an outdoor metallic sculpture he built, which aligned with the equinox and the solstice. The exhibit included an audio recording made by the wind affecting the sculpture and a documentary on its construction, together with a research report detailing a method of accurately calculating the mathematics of planetary orbits using geometry.

Circumstances have led Lindsay down different pathways in life. Earlier in his career, he became involved in the building construction industry. This provided a grounding in the communication required between architects, designers and builders, a necessary skill for producing the content in this book.

Restless by nature, Lindsay has travelled to 37 countries across all seven continents of the world. Combining this varied background with an artistic sensibility and lateral thinking, tempered by analytical logic, has enabled him to produce this ground-breaking work. This research both challenges and expands history's understanding of the Maya civilisation.

This book provides a solid foundation for Lindsay's chosen next stage in his life: to be a published author.